THE COMPLETE GUIDE TO
DECORATIVE LANDSCAPING
WITH BRICK & MASONRY

EDWARD J. HEDDY & PETE PETERSON

BETTERWAY PUBLICATIONS, INC.
WHITE HALL, VIRGINIA

Published by Betterway Publications, Inc.
P.O. Box 219
Crozet, VA 22932
(804) 823-5661

Cover design by Susan Riley
Typography by East Coast Typography, Inc.

Library of Congress Cataloging-in-Publication Data

Heddy, Edward J.
    The complete guide to decorative landscaping with brick & masonry /
Edward J. Heddy and Pete Peterson.
       p. cm.
    ISBN 1-55870-145-1 : $11.95
    1. Garden structures–Design and construction.   2. Building, Brick.
3. Masonry. I. Peterson, Pete. II. Title.
TH4961.H43   1990
717–dc20   89-29925
                                    CIP

Printed in the United States of America
0 9 8 7 6 5 4 3 2 1

We dedicate this book to every bricklayer and stonemason
— homeowner and professional —
who can stand back, look over a job just completed,
and say with pride, "I did that."

Credits and Thanks

Higgins Brick Company, 1845 South Elena Ave., Redondo Beach, CA.

Photograph on front cover: residence of David and Kris Brening, Agoura, CA.

Chicago Tribune Magazine for permission to reprint article, "I've Got Rocks in My House."

Illustrations by Kay Peterson and Jim Billman (Tools section).

Materials yard photos taken at Canoga Masonry Supply Co., Canoga Park, CA and Brening Building Materials Co., Van Nuys, CA.

Photographs by the authors.

Contents

SECTION III: APPENDIX

Introduction

Whether you live in a castle or a cottage, your home probably has some brickwork or masonry in evidence . . . if only a cinderblock foundation in your basement (or crawlspace) or a brick chimney. Unlike wood, which must be protected against the weather by periodic painting, brick and stone are more durable building materials, but they're certainly not impervious to wear. Even pyramids crumble and castles tumble, but a little do-it-yourself repair work will go a long way toward keeping your home intact. And it will save you a bundle. So that's what this book is partly about.

The other part of this book concerns how to build it yourself from scratch: brick walls, a fireplace, a patio walk, and lots more. Each chapter explains the basic, step-by-step procedures, pretty much the way I do it on the job. The photographs and illustrations make it even easier.

You don't need a raft of tools, either. Specialized tools, yes, but you don't need that many. And the ones you do buy will last forever. I'll tell you what's needed and show you what they look like.

Incidentally, all of the work outlined in this book can be handled by men or women–and a husband and wife team can halve the time and double the result.

Now, before you grab your trowel and start laying bricks, just a brief introduction.

My name is Ed Heddy. I grew up in Morris County, in northern New Jersey, and became a bricklayer's apprentice soon after I graduated from high school. After my first year I discovered the big problem with outdoor construction work in the East. It's the weather. In the winter you don't work.

Then the war caught up with me and I shipped out of Los Angeles with the U.S. Army, bound for the South Pacific. When we first arrived in L.A., in January, toward the end of World War II, the building boom in southern California hadn't gotten started yet; and I certainly didn't have a lot of free time (or money) to drive around the countryside. But I did notice that there was construction going on and that the weather was warm enough for bricklayers to be working outdoors. That certainly wasn't happening in January back in Morris County.

My trip to New Guinea took thirty-one days. During that time there wasn't much else to do except think, and all of my thoughts were focused on one resolve: If I came back alive, I would move to Los Angeles where a bricklayer could work outside twelve months a year. So that's what I did, and I also got caught up in the big building boom of the 50's and 60's which, in fact, is still going on.

I completed my apprentice program and worked with several contractors on a variety of jobs, but mostly building houses. Then I applied for a state license and started contracting on my own. In the 50's tract homes were the trend, hundreds of homes built one after another, at the same location. At first I did some of that work but I gradually began to concentrate on custom brick and stone work. I kept my company small and worked right alongside the men. I still do.

Then one year we did some stonework for a motion picture producer. He liked what I did and recommended me to one of his associates, who passed us along to the next guy and we began to do more than our fair share of work for the "movie crowd." Over the past forty years I've worked for singer

Tom Jones, John Wayne, Clark Gable, Maurice Jarre (who wrote the music for *Dr. Zhivago*), Rich Little, Henry Mancini, and many more.

They have more expensive houses than we do, but they're no more proud of their homes than you or I. And we always got along fine because in my line of work, I knew more than they did, which was why they hired me to do their remodeling.

Right now I'd like to share with you some of the things I've learned about brick and masonry. If you have a sizable job at your house, by all means hire a professional. But you'll be amazed at the things you can do yourself to keep your home in repair–and the money you'll save. The trick is knowing how to do the basics, and that's what this book is all about. After you finish a project, it's a great feeling to stand back, look it over and say, "Hey, I built that." I still get that feeling.

Section I
Fundamentals

EVERYTHING YOU WANTED TO KNOW ABOUT BRICKS AND THEN SOME

The History of Brick Making

In Joshua's time, the walls of Jericho were made of stone but most of the city itself was made of bricks. Compared with the long history of brick making, Jericho's "walls came a' tumblin' down" in relatively modern times. Almost ten thousand years ago, when the last ice age was ending, tribes were beginning to build permanent sites in that same region so that they could tend their crops of wild wheat and barley. Their early dwellings were made of sun-dried mud brick and over the millennia, handmade mud and clay bricks became literally the building blocks of civilization.

Recent archaeological diggings in the city of Ur have uncovered evidence that the Sumerians, who developed the first real civilization, also helped to preserve it through the use of weatherproof, kiln-fired brick. Of the Tower of Babel, the *Good News Bible* says: (Genesis 11:3) "The descendants of Noah came to a plain in Babalonia and settled there. They said to one another, 'Come on! Let's make bricks and bake them hard.' So they had bricks to build with and tar to hold them together. They said, 'Now let's build a city with a tower that reaches to the sky.'" The source of that tar is now part of the oil fields in modern day Iraq.

Early Egyptian paintings show scenes in a brick-yard with workers carrying clay and water which was then combined with straw or reed and mixed by other workers tramping it down with their feet. The mixture was formed in molds and burned or baked in the sun to make bricks which were often individually stamped with the reigning pharaoh's inscription. The ancient Chinese and Indian people also made brick in pretty much the same way. Much later, the Great Wall of China, which runs

for 2500 miles, was begun in the third century B.C. The outer walls were made of bricks with pounded earth and rubble forming the roadway between the supporting walls.

Brick making was probably introduced in Europe by the Greeks, but it was the Romans who developed brick making into an art. They were also the first to use mortar. Certainly the most celebrated bricklayer was the Prophet Mohammed who helped to lay bricks and build the structure that served as his dwelling and Muslim mosque soon after he arrived in Medina, in 622 A.D.

The use of bricks grew in popularity in England, especially for the most important structures, immediately after the great London fire in 1622. Even though wood was both inexpensive and readily available, brick making began in the Virginia and Massachusetts colonies as early as the 1630s.

The Spanish in Florida, starting in 1672, began building the fort of St. Augustine using a most unusual building material called coquina. This was quarried from beds of seashells — layer upon layer had accumulated under pressure over millions of years. It was soft and easily cut when wet, but very heavy. These waterlogged blocks were then hauled to the fort's limekiln where heat turned the seashell blocks into limestone solid enough to deflect cannonballs during the many sieges of the *Castillo de San Marcos*. The fort is one of the most popular tourist attractions at St. Augustine and its coquina blocks are still perfectly preserved.

Not too far away from the fort is what is said to be the oldest house in America, circa 1650, which also used coquina bricks for the original walls.

One celebrated bricklayer was Winston Churchill

BRICK SHAPE CHART

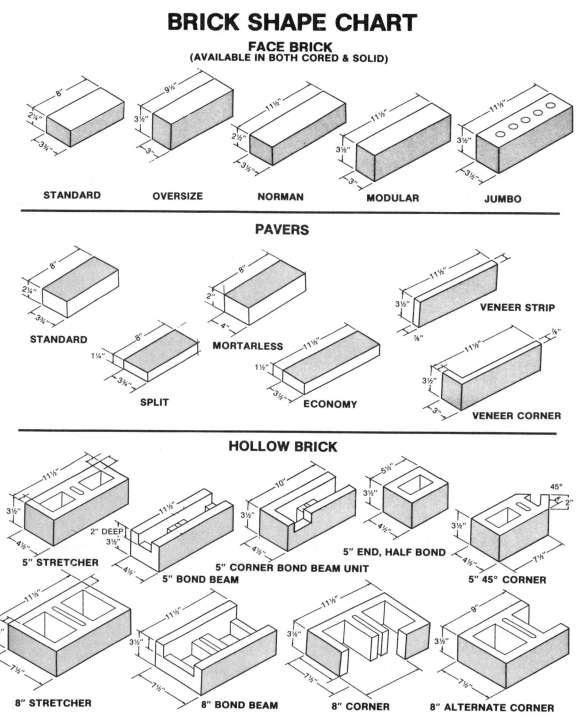

FACE BRICK
(AVAILABLE IN BOTH CORED & SOLID)

STANDARD   OVERSIZE   NORMAN   MODULAR   JUMBO

PAVERS

STANDARD   SPLIT   MORTARLESS   ECONOMY   VENEER STRIP   VENEER CORNER

HOLLOW BRICK

5" STRETCHER   5" BOND BEAM   5" CORNER BOND BEAM UNIT   5" END, HALF BOND   5" 45° CORNER

8" STRETCHER   8" BOND BEAM   8" CORNER   8" ALTERNATE CORNER

who did considerable brickwork at his estate, Chartwell. In his fascinating book, *The Last Lion,* William Manchester wrote: "James Scrymeour-Wedderburn, an early Chartwell guest, scribbled in his diary, 'Winston is building with his own hands a house for his butler, and also a garden wall.'

"He built much more than that. Altogether he finished two cottages, several walls, and a playhouse for Mary (his youngest daughter). Scrymeour-Wedderburn wrote: 'He works at bricklaying for hours a day, and lays 90 bricks an hour, which is a very high output.' He himself never claimed more than one a minute, but his craftsmanship was admirable; the sturdy results stand today.

"Churchill tried to join the Union of Building Trade Workers but after he received a certificate of membership and a union card, the Manchester local voted him ineligible."

Until relatively recent times, brick making was still a handmade operation, and even today the process is not much different from that followed centuries ago. The bricks are still made in standard sizes from the same materials and are not appreciably better in quality. Essentially, bricks are made of clay and fired in a kiln to make a weatherproof product that is unsurpassed in fire-resisting qualities, load-bearing strength, and is virtually impervious to heat and cold. Esthetically bricks add strength and dignity, as well as warmth and color to a structure. The construction brick was originally invented to fill a need and even today, thousands of years later, it hasn't been greatly changed or improved.

Kinds of Bricks

Bricks are made in virtually all parts of the world, and since soils differ in various geographies, so does the chemical composition of bricks. Essentially they are made of clay and shale burned in a kiln. There are many different types, some spe-cially designed for specific purposes, and most come in a variety of colors and textures.

Refer to the chart showing three types of bricks and their dimensions. (Courtesy Higgins Brick Co., Redondo Beach, CA.) You should keep in mind that actual brick sizes vary, so bear this in mind when figuring how many bricks to buy for a project. Also remember to allow for the mortar joint.

There are four types of brick that will handle virtually every homeowner job: common or building brick, face or veneer brick, paver brick, and firebrick.

COMMON — Usually red or pink (but you can get them in various colors and shades), measures $2\frac{1}{4}'' \times 3\frac{3}{4}'' \times 8''$, comes in several textures, three grades of hardness. These grades are:

SW — for severe weather (use in projects where bricks come in contact with the ground);

MW — for medium weather (projects subject to freezing but not in contact with the ground);

NW — for no weather (use for indoor work).

Common or building bricks are usually solid but can also be purchased with hollow cores. These provide a better bond and are slightly lighter in weight.

FACE BRICK — Better quality than common brick and used on outside walls for residential and commercial buildings. Some manufacturers also make a split veneer for both interior and exterior use. This is often applied with a mastic.

PAVER BRICK — Used for walks, driveways, and patios; designed for heavy traffic.

FIREBRICK — Used as a lining for fireplaces and barbecues; made of special clay fired at high temperatures to make it extremely heat resistant.

HOLLOW BRICK — Used in the construction of walls in place of concrete blocks.

CRUSHED BRICK — A building material that is used for walkways, roofing, and landscaping. It can be purchased in 40- and 80-pound bags.

USED BRICK — This is a completely different category and is exactly as the name suggests. More than that, it must be *old* used bricks, or at least bricks from demolished buildings or walls which were constructed at least forty years ago. Bricks before this time were usually laid with mortar made of sand and lime. The use of cement in mortar makes cleaning used brick too costly for practical use because the mortar is actually harder than the brick.

Used brick is generally cleaned with a hatchet at a salvage yard and sold in lots of 500 to a pallet-load.

Manufactured used brick is a good alternative if authentic used brick is not available. These are new bricks, often seconds or damaged bricks, which are painted or stained to resemble used brick and usually sold at the same price as new brick.

TOOLS USED IN MASONRY

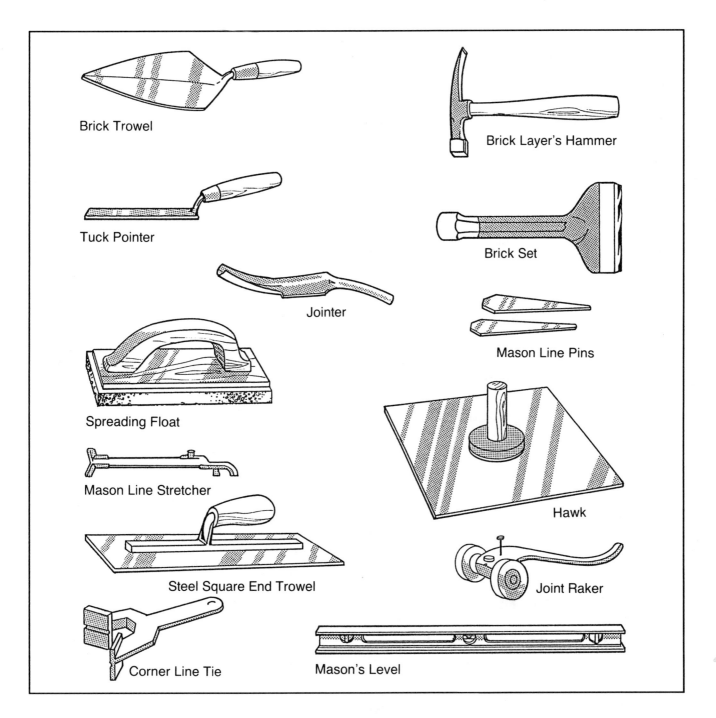

Brick Trowel

Brick Layer's Hammer

Tuck Pointer

Brick Set

Jointer

Mason Line Pins

Spreading Float

Hawk

Mason Line Stretcher

Steel Square End Trowel

Joint Raker

Corner Line Tie

Mason's Level

A WALK THROUGH A MASONRY MATERIALS YARD

If you have never been to a masonry materials yard, it might be an interesting experience to stop by and look around. At the very least the visit will introduce you to the wide choice of materials you have when you plan your next project. The scenes shown here are from commercial yards in the San Fernando Valley, which cater to subcontractors who do both residential and commercial work. They generally open at 7 a.m., six days a week.

Most of the contractors come in first thing in the morning, so you shouldn't choose that time for your visit. Usually after 10 a.m. the action has slowed down and the people at the yard will have time to handle your order or answer questions regarding anything that you see. (Long ago, I figured that it was smarter to pick up my materials on the way home to avoid the morning scramble. I also had a truck big enough to handle my next day's material.) Materials yards also carry bricklayer's tools and equipment — professional tools that will last a lifetime with just a little care. Bricklayers generally have their favorite materials yards depending on location and the kind of work they do.

Most homeowners have only used the brick and masonry materials that are carried by discount stores. These outlets are generally limited in the variety of materials they carry and usually sell no sand, gravel, or stone at all, unless it's bagged. So, if you plan to do any brick or stone work it might come in handy to know what's available at your neighborhood materials yard.

Sand, Gravel, and Crushed Rock

There are two basic types of sand: wash sand for use with concrete, and a product we call dry plaster sand, which is used for brick and block work. Whichever type is used, the grains must be sharp to provide a good bonding. Sea sand can never be used.

Gravel comes in many diameters; I prefer the ⅜-inch size, called pea gravel. It's easy to work with and most concrete pumps can only handle ⅜ inch gravel in residential concrete pouring jobs.

Crushed rock is ¾ inch or larger. Most state and federal work requires this for highways and bridges. The ready-mix truck must have a special pump in order to handle concrete made with ¾ inch crushed rock.

Bricks

Used bricks were originally laid with sand and lime in buildings prior to 1935. Today's mortar is harder than the brick. Used bricks are pleasing to the eye and are more expensive than new because they must be cleaned by hand with a hammer. There is also a manufactured used brick.

Common bricks are sold on pallets in 500 lot units, but you can buy them by the single brick if you want. They are fired in a kiln — often a million at a time — under strict quality control. Most bricks are made locally because of the shipping weight, and the quality of the brick will depend greatly on the condition of the local clay.

Slumpstone Blocks

Slumpstone blocks are made to resemble adobe blocks for a Spanish effect. They are used for walls and buildings and used in place of ordinary concrete block. Slumpstone comes in a variety of sizes and earth colors.

Flagstone

Flagstone is used mainly for patios and walks. Various names and kinds are available in every locality. The type shown here is Bouquet Canyon, so called because that's where it is quarried.

Broken Concrete

If you've wondered what they do with broken pieces of concrete from walks and driveways, well, they sell it. One example is for garden walls, placed in courses with the broken edges exposed. Often soil is packed in between the courses and various plants are added. You can also lay the pieces in mortar or use soil and plant with low growing plants.

Stone for Veneering

Stone for veneering comes in cut or rubble varieties and is sold by the pallet load. Veneering is laying stone or bricks over walls or block walls for esthetic purposes. Cut stone is laid in a pattern; rubble is odd shapes and sizes and is laid pretty much like a jigsaw puzzle.

Rebar

Reinforcing steel or rebar comes in 20-foot lengths for commercial use but can be cut into any size you want. Diameter sizes range from ¼ inch to 1 inch. Concrete block walls usually require from ⅜ to ¼-inch steel. Retaining walls can use from ½ inch to a full inch, which is also used in bridges and heavy construction work. The steel, embedded in concrete, is what gives a wall or structure the strength for withstanding shock and stress.

Concrete Block

Shown here being loaded on pallets by a forklift, concrete blocks are used in building construction and walls of all types. They come in various sizes, ranging from 4 to 16 inches wide. Because of the danger of earthquakes, 2-core blocks are probably more commonly used in California than anywhere else. A 2-core 6-inch block allows a sufficient mass of poured concrete around lengths of reinforcing steel that will provide ample strength for a garden wall. Depending on the height, a retaining wall must meet much more severe code restrictions, and you should check with your building inspector for this information.

Mexican Tile

Used for patios and walks, 12″ × 12″ Mexican tile is made of earth, generally kilned by wood fires. Because it's a soft product, it needs a couple of applications of plastic hardener for the best, longest lasting results.

Sand, gravel, and crushed rock.

Bricks.

Slumpstone blocks.

Flagstone.

Broken concrete.

Stone for veneering.

Rebar.

Concrete block.

Mexican tile.

HOW TO MIX MORTAR

Mortar is used to bond bricks or blocks. It is a mixture of cement, sand, lime, and water. Mortar has a second but important function of acting as a cushion to even out the irregularities of bricks and thus even out the load support. When properly bonded, mortar helps the brick surface become essentially waterproof and airtight. Another function is esthetic: Professional-looking mortar joints break up the monotony of a stack of bricks and make a brick wall or veneer surface truly a thing of beauty. More about that later.

You shouldn't confuse mortar with concrete, which is a mixture of cement, sand, water, and gravel. Concrete is a building material in itself, generally used for foundations, floorings, sidewalks, driveways, stairs, etc.

Portland cement generally comes in a one cubic foot paper sack weighing 94 lbs. (Be careful that you don't strain your back loading, or even worse *unloading,* sacks of cement from the luggage compartment of your car.) It is a mixture of cement and hydrated lime (chemically combined with water). You should remember that dry cement readily absorbs water, so don't store your bags on a concrete floor. It's best to keep them off the ground on a sheet of plastic on a pallet or at least a sheet of plywood. You should also check to make sure the bags haven't hardened on the bottom when you buy them, although bouncing them around a bit usually loosens them up.

You might think sand is sand, but there is as much difference in sand as there is in soil. To make good mortar the sand should be screened; the coarse grains should have sharp edges and be clean. If the grains are too fine the mix is difficult to work with because it dries out fast. Sea sand should not be used because salt in the sand will cause the mortar to crumble. Never use it! The best bet for the homeowner working on a small job is to buy sand by the bag from a brickyard or building supply store. This will be dry, of course. If you buy it by the ton it will probably be delivered wet which will affect the amount of water you will need for mixing.

White silica sand is also available and is generally used for laying tile or for matching existing white joints. In our part of the country it comes in several grades numbered 12, 16, 20, 30, 90, 150, and glass sand. The higher the number, the finer the grade.

To make a color mortar you simply add a small amount of dry color which you can buy in a materials yard or even from a commercial ready-mix plant. It comes as a powder in one-pound (or smaller) bags and a small amount will go a long way. When matching existing joints it's usually best to make a sample batch first. Then rub a small amount on the edge of a brick where it will quickly dry and indicate the shade you have mixed. If it's not exactly right, adjust accordingly. Be careful handling the dry color. If it blows around it will leave a stain wherever it lands.

Mixing Mortar

Most authorities advise 1 part (or bag) of Portland cement to 3 parts (or bags) of sand and enough water to make a mix about the consistency of oatmeal. You will get a softer mix and one that sets up more slowly if you add a shovelful of lime. If you are mixing concrete, don't add the lime. If you use a ready-mix add half a shovelful of cement to get a richer mix.

Mixing mortar is not a difficult task. First, mix the dry ingredients together with a hoe or flat-tip shovel. Then add a small amount of water and drag the dry materials into the water. Add additional water sparingly. It's easier to add more water than more dry materials in the proper proportions. When the mixture looks about right, make little cuts or ridges in your mortar with a trowel. If they look dry, add a very small amount of water; if they settle back and don't hold their shape, you have too much water.

It's a good idea to measure the ingredients until you get the hang of it. When he's on the job, laying bricks, a professional can tell by the feel if the mixture is too rich or too poor. Too much sand causes the mortar to drop off the trowel. The homeowner's best bet is to measure and be sure it's just right.

If you have a small job, such as tuckpointing, it might be handier for you to buy a masonry mix product and just add water. This costs more but it's more convenient. However, it's my belief that there is not enough cement in these products and, as I mentioned earlier, I add a half shovelful of cement to a 60-pound bag. (Note: Too rich mortar is as bad as not rich enough.)

Temperature is a factor. In the summer, with a temperature of 90 degrees or more, mortar will start to harden within an hour. At 50 degrees it will take a couple of hours. You should not allow it to freeze because that destroys the bonding qualities.

WHAT DO YOU MIX IT IN?

For most jobs, I use a power cement mixer which I haul behind my supply truck. When the mortar is mixed, we dump the mortar into a mason's wheelbarrow. For smaller jobs, we hand mix in a mortar box. This is a 3' × 5' metal box with sloping sides. You can make one out of wood or buy a small plastic container such as a 2' × 4' kids' wading pool. You can also use a wheelbarrow. A high-sided mason's wheelbarrow is worth buying (or renting) if you plan to do much work or have an ongoing project.

Remember to wash your mixing containers and tools thoroughly with a hose after using.

Masons and bricklayers use a specially designed hoe with two holes in the blade for hand mixing mortar, but an ordinary steel garden hoe will work almost as well. A square-tipped shovel can also be used. A pointed shovel might make it more difficult to avoid streaks in the mortar but if that's all you have, by all means, use it.

When your mortar is properly mixed, put a shovelful or two on a mortar board for easy access while laying bricks. You can easily make one out of a 3-foot square piece of 1-inch exterior plywood. Nail a 2″ × 4″ stud on two opposite sides to raise it off the ground or just place it on concrete blocks.

HOW MUCH SHOULD YOU MIX?

One bag of Portland cement with three bags of sand properly mixed with water will make enough mortar to lay about 100 bricks. One bag of premixed cement/sand will lay about forty bricks . . . probably enough for a small homeowner job.

Concrete Mixers

RENT THE SIZE YOU NEED

If you have a small job to do, a wheelbarrow, hoe, and shovel will work fine, but for a larger job it might be worthwhile to rent a power mixer. It probably doesn't make sense to buy one unless you plan to go into the business. Mixers come in three basic sizes: one-third sack, half sack, and full sack. The one-third sack mixer would be good for mixing concrete for a walk or an approach to a garage. The best approach is to tell the salesperson at the rental yard exactly what you are planning to do and follow his advice. (Of course, the sizes he has available will be a factor, too.)

In our part of the country, a one-third sack mixer rents for about $35 per day, a half sack for $50, and a full sack for $65. The names are misleading because you can mix a full sack of Portland cement in a half sack mixer and add 25 shovelsful of sand, which will give you a good batch of mortar. However, the one-third sack size mixer won't hold any more than that. A full sack mixer will handle two bags of cement and 50 or 55 shovelsful of sand, but you would probably need help to dispose of that amount of mortar before it gets stiff on you.

MIXING

Using a mixer requires a different procedure than mixing mortar by hand. Here you put the water in *first*. If you put in the cement first it will adhere to the sides of the mixer. (If cement gets stuck in the back of the mixer, the only way to get it out is with a hammer and chisel.)

Let's say you rented a half sack mixer. This is the procedure to follow.

- Turn the barrel to about a 35 or 40 degree angle.
- Turn on the mixer. (NOTE: Keep the mixer turned on all the time.)
- Throw in 5 gallons of water. (I use a 5-gallon plastic bucket.)
- Throw in 15 shovels of sand.
- Add a full bag of cement and
- Add an additional 10 shovels of sand.
- Add water as needed.

Now let the mixer go to work. Let it run for five minutes. You'll probably have to add more water. I can't be precise here because sand has different moisture contents and you'll have to experiment for the first load. (By remembering how much water you used with your first load, you'll be able to eliminate guesswork on your subsequent mixes.)

However, before you do add water, take a sample to see if your mortar is properly mixed. Lay a shovelful on a flat surface and see if you can raise a ridge or "comb," as we call it. Build a small pile until it flattens out. For work around the house, a good average would be a 4″ to 6″ slump. It should be stiff but not *too* stiff to work (which it probably is at this point, and if so, add enough water and test the slump again).

When you pour into your wheelbarrow, make sure that you have a good grip on the handle because the barrel is heavy; there's a lot of pressure working against you. Turn slowly and dump. The mix described above will fill my wheelbarrow twice. After I pour the first load, I add one quart of water and let the machine continue mixing for two minutes. Then shut off the machine while you use the first load of mortar.

NOTE: You can turn off the mixer and leave mortar in the barrel safely for at least thirty minutes. So, after you have removed a wheelbarrow load and if you know that you won't need another load for about fifteen or twenty minutes, you can shut off the mixer. Obviously, you should keep track of your time. Before starting up the mixer again, turn the barrel up straight. This will ease the tension on the motor and reduce the chance of blowing the breakers or fuse on your electrical system as it starts. When it's started, turn the barrel to the "mix" position. Also check for consistency and add a small amount of water if needed.

HOW TO MIX CONCRETE

You will probably need the full sack size mixer if you plan to pour concrete. Here you'll need 1 bag of Portland cement, 3 bags of sand, and 3 bags of pea gravel or ¾″ crushed rock (or the equivalent in shovels). It will certainly be worth your while to rent a mixer because most ready-mix companies really don't like to send out short loads. Understandably, they'd rather deliver a 7 to 9 yard load, and they could keep you waiting all day until they get around to your order, especially if it's a small one. In addition, you pay a premium for the short load. At least that's the way it works in my part of the country.

I specified pea gravel because it's what I prefer. You can use other types but pea gravel is easier to use, easier to shovel, and easier to finish.

- Throw in a 5-gallon bucket of water.
- Add 1 bucket of Portland cement.
- Add three 5-gallon buckets of sand and
- Three 5-gallon buckets of pea gravel.

Then let the machine mix and add one more bucket of water. After about five minutes of mixing take a sample and test your concrete to get the same kind of slump as descibed for mortar.

Occasionally we do a small patch job in the street or sidewalk for the city. The city requires a specific mix so I don't take any chances or shortcuts. If your work doesn't pass inspection, you tear it out — at your expense — and do it over.

The city requires a certain slump which might be a good standard for you to follow. The more water you add, the weaker the mortar or concrete will become, so city contracts specify the amount of water to be used. The inspectors require the same slump test described in the section on mortar. They have you lay out the concrete on a flat surface to see how high you can raise a comb before it collapses or slumps out. Different jobs have different specifications but, here again, a 4 to 6 inch comb is a good working average.

MAKE ENOUGH BUT NOT TOO MUCH

This holds true with mortar and concrete. Don't mix more than you can use in half an hour. When mortar or concrete stands around too long it gets stiff. On a job requiring inspection, we are generally allowed to add water once to make the mortar or concrete pliable after it has been standing

around, but if you do that often, it weakens the bond and loses its strength.

IMPORTANT: After you are finished mixing mortar or cement, clean out the machine thoroughly with a hose and water. Don't put it off until later because once cement hardens it has to be chipped off with a hammer. Also clean your wheelbarrow and hand tools.

GAS OR ELECTRIC?

A cement mixer is built ruggedly to last, so there are a lot of relics being rented out in the materials yards, and you might have to take what is available. I prefer the electric models and have three, along with a portable generator in the event I can't reach current. If you have a choice, use the electric mixer. It's a lot easier to start and if something is wrong you know it's not just being temperamental, as gasoline mixers frequently are.

My bias goes back to when I first got started in the business, in northern New Jersey. I had a pickup truck, a metal mortar box, and a couple of wheelbarrows, the necessary hand tools, and that's about it. Have trowel, will travel. One day a client wanted me to put in some stone steps and do a little patio work. As I was working, I noticed that he had an old mixer parked behind his garage. He said he bought it for a job and no longer had any use for it. So we made a trade and I thought I was ready to put in my bid to build the George Washington Bridge.

I was one of the few subcontractors in the area with a mixer. I'd leave it on the job until the work was finished and thought so much of it that I used to remove the wheels and set it up on blocks so nobody could drive off with it. It was a gasoline mixer with a mind of its own. I could run it all morning, then shut it off for lunch. And, of course, it wouldn't restart. Not for kicks or curses. I still have trouble with gasoline-powered mixers. They don't have electric starters; you have to wrap a rope around the pulley and yank on that. When it doesn't start, you blame yourself rather than the machine, which makes it even more frustrating.

In summary: If you have an amount of mortar or concrete to mix, you could save money by renting a mixer. Estimate how much mortar or conrete you need and talk it over with the salesperson at the materials yard. Compare the effort of mixing by hand with the convenience of renting a mixer.

Then, if you're pouring concrete, compare the cost of renting a mixer with the cost of buying from a ready-mix supplier.

On a professional job, for both efficiency and economy, the rule of thumb is one helper for two working bricklayers. I've worked alone with a mixer at home, but I can tell you, it's a lot better to have a helper. For the average homeowner it is essential.

PAINTING ON BRICK AND MASONRY

Brick

As a bricklayer, I'm biased, of course. I think a natural brick surface is beautiful as it is. If it is still natural brick, think carefully before painting because it is next to impossible to remove the paint once it's on the siding. New brick carries paint better than used brick because there are fewer bleeding salts and acids to affect the paint. However, brick can be painted successfully and both professional painters and homeowners do it often. You probably have seen painted brick homes in your neighborhood.

If your brick house (or side) has already been painted, there's no decision; eventually it must be repainted. Flat latex, or water base, paint is better than a glossy oil finish paint. Oil finish, or alkyd, paint tends to highlight the imperfections, whereas flat latex tends to hide them. Use two coats of flat latex. The easiest way to paint brick is with a long nap roller or by spraying.

Stucco

Stucco is a mixture of cement, sand, and lime that usually has a rough, sand-like texture which can be painted or left in a natural condition, especially if color has been added to the original mixture. If the surface has deteriorated or is soft and crumbly to your fingernails, you should use a masonry conditioner, then apply a flat latex paint of whatever color you choose. Since it's a flat paint, you can use a second coat if you feel it's needed. (Just don't paint a coat of gloss over gloss.) Stucco is best painted with a long nap roller or sprayer.

NOTE: Often stucco just needs to be washed rather than painted. The best way to do this is with a power washer. CAUTION: If you rent a power washer, make sure you're thoroughly checked out on it. They can be hazardous to use unless you know what you're doing. The powerful jet stream of water can easily break windows.

Foundations

The foundation of a house is often referred to as "blockwork" and as far as painting is concerned, it is almost as important as the siding. In older homes, the foundations are often made of stone. If it has never been painted and it's properly tuck-pointed, by all means, leave it as is. But if the material is concrete block, poured concrete, or block covered with stucco, it will probably improve the overall appearance of the house if it is painted, especially if much of the foundation shows. Whatever the material, it is usually much rougher than the siding, so it's important to use a flat paint — an exterior flat latex. Have the paint store tint the shade needed to blend into the body of the house or to contrast with it. If two coats are needed, use the same paint for both.

Patio Decks

Don't try to paint a patio deck, especially with an oil-base paint, which won't dry properly. Use a specially formulated patio paint which is a chemical dye that etches into the surface to provide a much longer-lasting coverage than a flat paint.

Sealing

Brick veneer, walks, steps, or planters can be effectively sealed and mortar joint crumbling slowed down a great deal with the simple application of Thompson's Water Sealer. The easiest way to do this is to buy or rent a Hudson sprayer, or an equivalent backpack-type sprayer. Just mix in the sealer, according to the instructions, pump up the pressure as directed, and spray the bricks.

I use an easy trick to get traction on brick steps by sprinkling a little silica sand on the steps before the water sealer dries. Incidentally, if you live in the snowbelt, one of the worst things you can do to your brick, stone, or concrete steps and walks is to use salt to melt the ice.

USING SCAFFOLDING

Scaffolding is to the bricklayer what a ladder is to a painter: a means to work safely above ground level. However, scaffolding provides more than just a place to place your feet. A painter can work with one hand holding his brush and the other hanging onto the ladder, but a bricklayer must use both hands for brick and trowel. And while a pothook can secure the paint bucket to the ladder, the bricklayer must work with a pile of bricks and a supply of mortar at his feet, so the scaffolding must be sturdy enough to support the additional weight and the worker's movement.

I should also mention at this point that it is illegal in California for a bricklayer to work from a ladder. And even if it's not illegal in your state, it's unsafe; that's an even better reason for not doing it.

Scaffolding, when disassembled, is simply a number of heavy gauge steel tubing units and 4″ × 4″ steel pads used as supports to keep the legs from sinking into the ground. There are two basic kinds: residential and commercial. When assembled, residential is essentially made of 5′ high × 7′ wide × 5′ deep sections; commercial is 6′8″ high × 7′ wide × 5′ deep sections. For most homeowner work the residential scaffolding is more convenient. But if you're renting your scaffolding, you'll have to take what's available.

Setting Up Residential Scaffolding

The basic section of scaffolding consists of two crossbraces (the front and back units) and two jacks (the side units), which have a built-in metal ladder, or steps, about 16 inches apart. There are also four footpads.

First, check your ground level. If it is level, fit one footpad on each leg. If the ground slopes, the scaffold will lean in toward the wall or away from it. To make it level and safe for working, adjust one or more legs with 2″ × 10″ sections of planks. The inside of the assembled scaffold should be about two inches from your working wall.

Each unit — crossbraces on front and back, jacks on sides — fastens together. Most have lock-on devices, secured with pins; some bolt or snap together. Each assembled four-sided section provides the building block for the next section, at the ground level or the second story, if and when you go higher. All sections interlock with each other.

The purpose of the scaffold, of course, is to provide a working base to stand on and work from. This base is planking and each plank is a full two inches thick, by code, and 10 inches wide. The ends have a ¼-inch bolt running through them to prevent the plank from splintering if it is dropped — which you should *never* do. Hand the planks down to a helper or lean them against the sides of the scaffold. The standard length is 10 feet; plasterers also work with a 16-foot length. The length is important because if you have two sections, side by side, there should be a one foot overlap on each side.

Before starting to assemble, check each plank for damage. The metal scaffold units are welded and these should be checked as well. (Under the California code, manufacturers must use state-certified welders.)

Most bricklayers put two planks on the third step on either side of the jacks (three won't fit). The third step is just below the top bar. They then work at this height. They put three or four planks on the top bar behind them for storing their bricks and mortar and this way reduce their bending.

Commercial Scaffolding

In addition to being higher (6'8" vs. 5'), the assembled commercial scaffolding section allows you to walk through it. The residential units have steps which prevent this. The scaffolding is assembled the same way as the residential type with two major differences. There is a railing at the top to keep you from falling, and you'll need a ladder to climb up to the working area. This ladder must be secured to the scaffold. When disassembling the scaffold, all planks should be handed down to a helper or lowered with a rope.

Residential scaffolding showing front and back crossbraces and side jacks. Steel pads are on planking to adjust for ground slope.

Planking added to support bricklayer and mortar table (top).

Commercial scaffolding with outrigger.

HOME REPAIRS: SHOULD YOU HIRE A PROFESSIONAL OR DO IT YOURSELF?

There is no all-purpose answer to this question, of course, because there are too many variables. The question must be job specific to begin with. Then the homeowner must decide. Are you ready, willing, and able to take on the project? Must it be done now (within a certain time limit), or can it be accomplished during your free time? And how valuable is your "free time"? Do you enjoy working with your hands? Are you physically up to it? Does the job *have* to be done? And, not the least important, can you afford to have it done?

Here are a few considerations that might help you decide. "Home repairs," as used here, can be applied to work involving any of the trades and skills — painting, plumbing, carpentry, electrical work, or whatever — not just those related to brick and masonry.

Hire a Professional

1. The job will be done properly. This is especially important if the work requires specialized skills (such as electric wiring or plumbing), or must be approved by a local building inspector. It might even be hazardous unless done by an expert.

2. The job will be done now, and in its entirety, or at least within your agreed-upon schedule. Many homeowners start a job and never get around to completing it. Can you afford *not* to finish it?

3. Are you physically able to handle the job? You don't have to be a little old lady to have difficulty with many strenuous jobs--building a concrete block wall, for one.

4. If the job requires specialized training, skills, or talent, it might be cheaper in the long run to hire a professional.

Do It Yourself

1. You'll probably save money. A good many jobs around the house are labor intensive. If you can provide that labor you'll often save a significant amount of money.

2. It's rewarding to do it yourself. Most of us get a tremendous lift to look back at a job we accomplished and say, "Hey, not bad. I did that myself." Even after working a lifetime in the brick and masonry trade, I still get that feeling. When I don't, I'll quit.

3. Often there's no choice. If a job must be done and you quite simply have more outgo than income, you've just volunteered yourself for a project.

4. Sometimes you can do it better yourself, especially if a project must be done in parts and pieces over a period of time, or it must sync with another schedule or condition. This way you can take the time to do it right without compromise or shortcut.

All things considered, the most important variable in the equation is the lifestyle and attitude of the individual homeowner. Some of us like doing things with our hands. Some of us secretly enjoy the reputation of being something of a klutz. And even those of us who are handy often have jobs we hate to do. For instance, I wouldn't mow a lawn if I were threatened with a gun. "Why? It will only grow back." When I do something I want it to last. Like building a garden wall.

Building Permits

Building codes vary from one town or city to the next, but one thing is constant: If you are building, remodeling, or substantially changing the exterior or interior of your home, you will need a building permit. Home improvement repairs, such as building a brick barbecue or resurfacing your patio, may or may not require such a permit. The only way to be sure is to check your municipal building code. Your local Building Permit & Inspections Department is probably listed under City Government in the phone directory. Most likely there is no printed list detailing what is and isn't permitted. Instead, your specific request for information is usually treated on an individual basis. Often the homeowner is asked to "come in and describe what it is you would like to do," or, for a larger project, "show us your plans and blueprints."

The specifics of what does and does not require a permit might often seem illogical. In some localities, for example, if you install replacement windows of the same window opening size, no permit is required, but if the new windows are several inches larger (or smaller) you might have to get a building permit. However, modern vinyl-clad replacement windows often use up much more space for the frame than older windows. Thus, the glass area might be greatly reduced and even though the opening was the same size, the replacement could have a substantially different look.

The prudent approach will be to assume that you *will* need a permit. Therefore, early in the planning stages, phone or visit your municipal building department and describe your project. And even if you plan to hire a contractor or professional to do the work, don't assume that he will routinely have obtained the permit. Do some inquiring on your own first.

Generally, however, if you do hire a professional, it will be a good approach to discuss the permit and ask him to handle it. He's done it before and knows the procedure. He can often eliminate the delays and cut through the red tape that exists in some offices. In a small office, for example, the person who handles the permits might also be the inspector who is often out in the field. For this and other reasons, the homeowner is advised not to wait until the last minute before checking on or obtaining the building permit.

There are additional reasons for learning about building permits. For example, if you are living in a district zoned for historic preservation, the restrictions on what you can and can't do are often rigidly controlled. A different color coat of paint than currently exists on your home could cause a problem, and a permit to install a vinyl-clad replacement window in an old Victorian house might well be denied. Zoning regulations might also be a consideration before going ahead with your project. So is any work that might affect your neighbors.

If you live in a rural area, such basic necessities as drilling a well or installing a new septic system will certainly require a health department permit and follow-up inspection.

It probably goes without saying that anything pertaining to plumbing and electricity, and usually heating and ventilation, will have to be inspected. Plumbers and electricians are well aware of this and the necessity of an inspection ensures the integrity of the job and protects the homeowner from improper work. The absence of such inspection could very well affect the future sale of the house and provoke a fine. In short, it's for your own protection to conform with the local building code regulations: to get your permit, have it inspected, if that's what it takes, and get on with the next job. "Don't fight city hall" is still a valid piece of advice.

On some projects it will be necessary for the building inspector to come out to your home and inspect the site before the construction begins. Other jobs might require inspections at certain stages during the construction, and there is often a final inspection. The fees that are charged for the building permit go toward paying the inspectors to do their job. Fees vary greatly and can range from a simple, flat $3 or $5 price for the permit, or you can be charged from 2 to 8% of the anticipated cost of the project. The burden is on the homeowner to report the anticipated work.

The basic reasoning behind the necessity of getting a building permit (and sometimes an inspection when the job is completed) is, in a word, *safety*. The purpose is to protect the homeowner currently living in the house, and also a prospective buyer who may someday purchase that house. Your home must meet the prevailing building codes in your municipality . . . whether you voted for them or not. And any changes that you make must also conform. But there's another reason for city hall wanting to know what improvements you make. Your taxes may be increased.

A DOZEN TIPS ON STARTING A NEW JOB

Most of these tips are common sense reminders of things you've already thought about. Even so, I can almost guarantee that one of them will save you time and money if you run through the list before you start. And don't forget to use the work forms scattered throughout this book.

1. **Building Codes.** Call or visit the Building Permit and Inspections Department that has jurisdiction in your locality. Do this while your project is still in the planning stage. Even though it's your property, and the job is probably not a major renovation, the odds are that you will need to get a permit. It's also possible that your work will be inspected to make certain that it meets code requirements. City Hall usually holds that it's your responsibility to apply for building permits and to conform with municipal standards. If you need a building permit you will be charged a fee.

2. **Neighbors.** Do your neighbors know what you are planning to do? Would it be a good idea to mention it? Will the work affect them in any way?

3. **Planning.** Think through your job before you start. Do you have a sketch or blueprint? Would it be helpful to have one? Is everything measured and staked out? Do you know exactly what must be done? Have you figured out the necessary steps in order of completion?

4. **Materials.** Do you know what materials you need? Do you have a written list? Do you know the exact quantities, types, and sizes? Do you know where to buy the material you need? Can you get everything from one source? (It might be cheaper to shop around, but you'll probably save in the long run if you can get everything from one source.)

5. **Tools.** Do you have everything you need? Do you have to buy any new tools for this specific job? If it's an expensive tool, can you rent it or borrow it? Do you know where your tools are? Are they all together in one place, ready to begin work? (After you mix your mortar, it is frustrating to have to look for your trowel.)

6. **Equipment.** Do you need special equipment for this job? (A power mixer, for example, or scaffolding.) Do you know where to rent it? Can you be sure it will be available for the time period you need it?

7. **Help.** Do you have to hire professional help for the job? Have you gone over the job and discussed the helper's estimate? Will he be available when you're ready to start?

Do you plan on getting help from your relatives or neighbors? Do you have a firm commitment for the time you need them? Can you manage if your helpers have a change of plans?

8. **Stopping Work.** Do you have a stop-work point? If your job will take longer than one day, or a weekend, have you anticipated a point at which you can stop the job until next weekend . . . or longer? Can you cover your work safely, without danger to your family or your materials?

9. **Delivery.** Have you scheduled your materials to be delivered in time for your anticipated start? Will someone be at home to tell the driver where to leave the materials? It should be near your work site so you don't waste time

and energy moving materials or equipment. Have you made certain that the materials will be covered for protection against the weather? (This is especially important for bags of cement.)

Do you plan to pick up the necessary materials? Do you have to borrow a pickup truck or trailer to get them?

10. **Time.** Allow plenty of it. Unless you're experienced, the work will probably go slower than you anticipated. And unless you're in pretty good shape your muscles will be pretty weary at the end of the day. Handling bricks or concrete blocks is like working out with weights. Don't knock yourself out to finish the job. When you're working for yourself you've got a pretty good boss. He'll understand if you have to postpone some work until tomorrow.

Some homeowners approach a job with the thought of just getting it done. Don't! Work steadily but take it slow and easy. When you're working with brick or masonry, the job will probably last your lifetime. Do it right because if you do you should never have to repeat that same job again.

11. **Weather.** Since your job is probably outdoors, there is always the possibility that you'll be rained out. Do you have a contingency plan (apart from having a cold drink and waiting until the rain stops)?

12. **Insurance.** Are you covered should one of your friends or neighbors get hurt on the job while helping you out? Are you sure? You could be liable. Also make certain that any professional has proper insurance and is covered by worker's compensation when you hire him.

Section II Projects

BRICK WALL

TOOLS & MATERIALS NEEDED

- ☐ Wheelbarrow
- ☐ Mixing board
- ☐ Shovel
- ☐ Hoe (for mixing)
- ☐ Bricklayer's trowel
- ☐ Rat-tail jointer
- ☐ Level
- ☐ Mason's line and line block
- ☐ 2″ × 4″ studs
- ☐ Hammer and nails
- ☐ Sponge and half of sponge rubber ball
- ☐ Bricks
- ☐ Concrete
- ☐ Mortar

To construct a brick wall, follow the step-by-step instructions here, referring to the photographs on the following pages. For demo purposes we laid a footing alongside an existing driveway and built a wall 4 feet long and 5 courses high. The steps are the same for a wall of any height or length.

Lay a Footing

A concrete footing base is necessary to provide proper support for virtually every kind of brick walk. The first step is to stake out the length of your wall and to make sure it follows a straight line. Next, dig a trench. You want to end up with a poured concrete footing about 12 inches deep and 12 to 14 inches wide. However, the depth of your trench depends on the frostline in your area.

Check with your local building inspector for this information. If you must go below 2 feet, lay a foot of poured concrete and build up to just below the surface with concrete block to reduce the cost of the poured concrete footing. You'll have to use 12-inch wide (or deep) block because a two-course brick wall is 8 inches deep, and they don't make a standard 10-inch wide concrete block.

Concrete

If you mix the concrete yourself in a mixing box, the formula is 1 part (or bag) of Portland cement to 3 parts sand and 3 parts pea gravel mixed dry first, then combined with the proper amount of water. If your wall is more than 50 feet long, it will probably pay you in time and effort to order ready-mix (also called transit mix) concrete, even though you'll pay a premium for a short load. You must also make sure you have easy access for the ready-mix truck to pour into your trench. If not, you can order a pump which the ready-mix company will provide for an additional fee. Your other option is renting a cement mixer.

Pour the Footing

You don't need forms because your footing will be underground; however, the top must be level. To make sure it is level, you can set a 2″ × 4″ stud along the length of your trench, slightly below the surface of the soil. (Butt the studs together with splints on either side if you need more than one.) Hammer in 14-inch long wood stakes at 6-foot intervals in the bottom of the trench and secure the 2″ × 4″ stud(s) to these. The bottom plane of the 2″ × 4″ should be just below the surface of the soil, and

1. To provide proper support, a free-standing brick wall should be 2 stretcher courses wide, or one header brick (laid across) deep, for the even courses. Lay the end bricks first to start off the wall.

2. Lay a dry run to determine the position of the bricks at the other end of the wall. Mark position with a pencil.

3. Set your opposite end bricks and set up a mason's line. Use your level to make sure everything is true.

4. Lay the first course, one row at a time, using your mason's line as a guide.

5. Use a rat-tail jointer to strike the joints after each course. Do the head joints first, then the horizontal bed joints with long, continuous motion.

6. You can't butter the sides because you need to hold onto the brick. Fill in the joints between the rows later.

7. *Lay a header brick to start off the second course so your joints will be staggered.*

8. *Set both end bricks before starting to lay the second course. Set a mason's line as a guide and check with your level to make sure the course is true.*

9. *Bricklayers use a line block to set a mason's line but you need to add more mass to support the single header block, so it's a good idea to set the next two bricks at either end. We added additional bricks to show off the mason's line.*

10. Finish off the top course of a wall with header brick. Set two bricks at either end to provide weight and use a double mason's line so both sides of the bricks line up true.

11. The last brick laid is the closure brick. Butter both sides.

12. Clean off the sides of the wall with half of a dry sponge rubber ball.

you can use this as a guide for pouring. Use a mason's level to be sure it's true.

Pour the concrete up to, but not on, the 2″ × 4″s. It/they will be removed, but the stakes will remain embedded in the concrete. No problem. Use a wood float or piece of 2″ × 4″ for smoothing out the concrete. Let the footing dry overnight. (A bricklayer would probably lay the first course in the wet footing, but the homeowner would be well advised to wait until it's dry.)

Mix the Mortar

For your mortar, use the standard 1 part Portland cement to 3 parts sand with enough water to get the proper consistency. Don't make any more mortar than you can use in about a half hour. Depending on the size of your wall and your mixing container (mixing box or wheelbarrow), you might start out with a half bag of cement. If you have any lime, a shovelful will make the mortar work more easily. Mix the ingredients first, then add the water. Don't overwater. When you lay a bed of mortar (bricklayers call it "mud") on your footing for your first course, it should furrow and stay firm.

Wet Bricks

New bricks should be wetted down before using, but don't soak them. Dry bricks absorb the water in the mortar and cause it to crumble; soaked bricks leak water into the mortar, weakening it. I generally put a load of bricks in a wheelbarrow and dump water on them, then remove them from the wheelbarrow. If they're too wet they will look shiny, but they'll dry fast.

Lay the End Bricks

Cut off the stakes flush with the concrete, then lay a dry course of brick, using your finger as a guide to allow ½-inch space for your mortar joint. De-termine your beginning and end points and mark these with a pencil on your footing.

Set your first brick on a small bed of mortar, tap it gently into position, and level it both ways. Now go to the other end of the wall and repeat the process with your end mark. You know that your remaining bricks will fit between the end bricks because of your dry run. It's important that they do fit because you don't want a half brick in the middle of your wall.

Set a Mason's Line

Bricklayers use what is called a *line block* to hold their mason's line (which is really nothing more than a sturdy line that won't break easily). The line will be your guide to help you lay the rest of the course. If you have a couple of line blocks, set one at your end brick and pull the line taut and parallel with the tops of both bricks. Then use the other line block to hold the line in position. If you don't have line blocks, use a dry brick at either end (on top of your set bricks), and tie off both ends of your line. The important thing is to make sure the line is parallel to the bricks. If one of your bricks is slightly out of position, adjust it so it is parallel while the mortar is still damp.

An alternate way of lining up your first two bricks is to use the length of 2″ × 4″ that you used to pour the footing, but you'll still have to set a line for the rest of the course.

Lay the First Course

Your wall will be two bricks deep, but it will probably be easiest to do one row at a time. If you are right-handed, you might want to work left to right. Lay a bed of mortar on top of the footing, enough for about three bricks. Throw about a 2½-inch wide bed and use your trowel to drag the point down through the center, opening up the mortar into two furrows about 5 inches wide. This will be slightly more than the width of a 4-inch brick. This is called *frogging* because the pattern looks something like frog's legs.

Hold the brick in your left hand (if you're right-handed), and turn your hand. Hold the trowel in your right hand and put enough mortar on your trowel so you can "butter" the end of the brick. This is for the head joint. Place this brick into the bed of mortar, buttered end against your already set end brick. Use the end of your trowel to tap it into place, flush with the line. Your line tells you it's true horizontally, so use your level to check across. Tap to adjust. Both your head and bed joints should be about ½ inch deep.

Continue with the first course (actually the first row of the first course) until you are ready to lay the last brick. This is called the *closure* brick. You butter both ends of this brick and also butter the ends of the laid brick on either side of the closure brick. This will give you a full head joint on both sides and allows the brick to slip into place more easily. Tap it in place with your trowel handle and level it. Then remove the excess mortar. You should remove the excess mortar from the sides as you progress. This excess can be returned to the mortar board and reused.

Now you can repeat the action for the second row. Set the bed joint mortar as you did before; set a brick at either end to set your mason's line. However, there is one adjustment you'll have to make. When you set your first end brick, place it in the bed joint mortar but don't butter the end. You'll have to adjust the depth by placing a dry brick across the top to make sure your two rows are as wide as the width of one brick. (The end bricks on the second course use a header position — across the wall.)

When both end bricks of the second row have been laid, set your line on the top outside edge. Start to lay your bricks as you did before; butter the ends but don't butter the side of the brick. You need to hold onto it for one thing, for another, it's easier

to fill in the joint between the two rows after the course is completed.

Second Course

Next, lay the end brick at either end of the second course in the header position — across the wall. (This is to permit a staggered head joint between the courses.) The header bricks must be level and plumb on all four corners. Use your level both ways and set the line after both ends have been laid. If you don't have a line block, tie your line to a nail.

It's a good practice to strike your head and bed joints after you complete each course. Use an S-shaped rat-tail jointer to get a concave, finished look. (If you don't have one and don't want to buy one for a small job, you can make a serviceable tool out of what the electricians call "thin wall." This is thin flexible tubing that can easily be bent into an S-shaped pipe that you can use to make the concave joint.) To get a nice clean line, strike the head joint first and then, with a long continuous motion, make the horizontal bed joint. The concave joint seals the brick against the weather. You could improvise an S-shaped tool, but a rat-tail jointer allows you to apply the proper pressure.

Here again, start laying one row at a time for your second course. First the front, then the back row, and fill in the center joints when both rows are completed. Then repeat striking the joints. You don't have to strike the center joint. When you're laying your second brick, after your header has been laid, you should be careful not to put too much side pressure or you'll push the header out of plumb. The closure brick works the same on all courses.

The third course will revert back to the stretcher position for the ends. This alternate stretcher-header-stretcher pattern for the ends will continue throughout the wall. When you reach the top of the wall (we only used five courses high for our

demo wall) you can top off the wall with a header pattern to give a finished look to the job.

When you lay the top course you should lay two header bricks at each end before setting your line. That's to provide enough mass and weight so you don't knock the brick out of plumb. You should also tie two lines for this course — one for the front and the other in back so both sides of the header bricks line up true. Each brick must have a complete bed joint — all the way across the full depth of the wall. You'll also have to butter the sides of the bricks.

As you lay your courses you should use the head joints as a kind of running check so you don't have a surprise at the end of the wall. The head joints should line up with every third course; i.e., the first and third courses, the second and fourth courses should line up. If they are not lining up, use your mortar to make an adjustment so they do.

As mentioned, you should have sealed joints to weatherproof your wall; this is especially important on top. As you lay the top course, strike each joint with your rat-tail jointer as you go along. The closure technique is the same except that you are working with the brick lengthwise.

Clean the Wall

After the top course has been completed (on a small wall; long before that on a long wall), it's time to clean off the brick. The top of the wall, which has a rough surface, is best cleaned with a damp sponge. Repeat cleaning until all the mortar is removed. The sides are smoother, so they are best cleaned dry. If you can get one, the best thing to use is a half of a sponge rubber ball. Just rub dry

until the spots and stains are gone. If you can't find a sponge rubber ball, use a dry towel or a piece of burlap. Using water will cause a white cast to appear because of the salts in most water.

A couple of notes regarding the accompanying photographs. I built a small wall for demonstration purposes. We also used common bricks. These are cheaper in price than number one brick. Consequently, they have slight defects. You can use any kind of brick for your wall.

The Final Step

Clean up the area and your tools. If you follow instructions, you will have a wall you can be proud of; maybe one that Winston Churchill in his prime couldn't have done better.

SUMMARY

- Purchase bricks and materials.
- Dig a trench the length of the wall, 12 to 14 inches wide, 12 inches deep.
- Pour a concrete footing.
- Mix mortar; wet bricks.
- Lay end bricks, set mason's line.
- Lay first course, one row at a time. Strike your joints with rat-tail jointer.
- Lay second course; end bricks are headers.
- Finish courses, top off with header course. Strike joints on top.
- Clean the wall; sponge on top, half sponge rubber ball rubbed dry on sides.
- Clean up area and tools.

CONCRETE BLOCK WALL

TOOLS & MATERIALS NEEDED

- ☐ Concrete blocks (determine size) including channel blocks and caps
- ☐ Concrete
- ☐ Mortar (cement, sand)
- ☐ Rebar
- ☐ Spacers (for bottom of trench)
- ☐ Wood stakes
- ☐ 2″ × 4″ studs
- ☐ Hammer and nails
- ☐ Mortar mixing box
- ☐ Wheelbarrow
- ☐ Trowel
- ☐ Rat-tail jointer
- ☐ Mason's line
- ☐ Line stretcher

Often called cinderblocks, concrete blocks are most frequently used for walls and foundations. They're rugged, relatively inexpensive, fireproof, and easy to use for a homeowner project, even though the individual block weighs about 35 pounds and can run to 50 pounds. The best part is that once you pour your footing, you can start building, as fast or slow as you like.

Decorative blocks are also available in a variety of patterns and are often set in solid walls to add light and variety. They can also be used as a design or screen wall to provide privacy and atmosphere in front of a home.

Paver blocks, often interlocking, are frequently used to build walks and driveways.

Size of Concrete Blocks

The standard size is quoted at 8″ × 8″ × 16″, but the actual size is slightly less to allow for a $\frac{3}{8}$-inch mortar joint. Generally all concrete blocks are 16 inches long and 8 inches high, but the widths vary at 4, 12, and 16 inches.

The sizes used for most garden walls are either 4 or 6 inches wide. Blocks used for retaining walls and buildings are usually 8 inches wide, depending on the height and type of the wall. (You should check the municipal codes in your area.) For instance, on a retaining wall of more than 12 feet, the local code here states that the first 2 feet must be constructed with 16-inch wide blocks, the second 2 feet should reduce to 12 inches, and the remainder of the wall should use 8-inch wide blocks. In addition, most southern California construction uses 2-core, or 2-hole, blocks because of the strict codes written to provide protection against earthquakes. You can pack more concrete mass around a reinforcing rod in a 2-core block than you can in the 3-core block commonly used in most other parts of the country.

Dig a Trench and Set the Horizontal Support

A 6-inch wide wall will need a trench about 18 inches wide and 1 foot deep. You will also need a number of 2″ × 4″ studs; enough for the length of the wall. The bottom of this support should be level with, or slightly below, the top of your existing soil. It should be secured with stakes and set down the center of the trench. If you have to use more than one length, butt two pieces together and nail on a 1″ × 4″ splint on the outside. The stakes should be at least 2 feet long to provide the necessary support. Stake every 6 to 8 feet. The starting edge of your 2″ × 4″ should be fixed so that it will also be the starting edge of your first block.

Place Rebar

Place a piece of ⅜ inch rebar, or reinforcing steel, at the bottom of the trench to strengthen the footing. To avoid rust, and to make sure the steel is embedded in the concrete, use 3″ × 3″ concrete spacers. These are designed to support rebar and come with a piece of wire for tying; use as many as you need. If you require more than one piece of rebar, allow a 2-foot overlap and secure the overlap with wire.

Pour the Footing

If your wall is 25 feet long, for example, you would need a cubic yard of concrete. This is a bit much to mix by hand, even in a professional mixing box, so the homeowner has the option of renting a cement mixer, which would come in handy for mixing mortar later, or of buying a short load of ready-mix and paying a premium. It might be well to compare the prices. One factor will be accessibility for the ready-mix truck or the use of a pump (at an additional cost).

Fill the trench to the bottom of the 2″ × 4″ support, but don't cement it in because that will be removed after the footing has been set. The stakes can remain embedded and will be cut off at the top of the form.

Buy Blocks

Determine the length of the wall. The easiest way is to tell the materials salesperson the length and height of your wall and he'll tell you how many blocks you will need. As a rule of thumb, for a 24-foot wall you'll need 18 blocks per course. Figure two half blocks every other course and omit one

block. (The second course equals 17 blocks plus 2 half blocks.) As a reminder, regardless of the size block you're using, all block is heavy . . . some are just heavier than others, especially when you have to lift them up over a vertical rebar. You might also want to use gloves for handling them.

Have your sand and gravel delivered with your blocks. Your materials salesperson will help you figure the amount. As a reference, you'll need about 1500 pounds of sand, depending on the moisture in the sand, and the same weight of gravel.

Make a Dry Run

The next day (or work session) after you pour the footing, lay out the first course of blocks dry. Mark your footing at each end with a pencil and make sure your blocks fit between the end pieces, allowing about ⅜ inch for mortar between each block. Adjust until you're sure everything fits.

Mix Mortar

If you rented a mixer for your concrete, by all means use it for the mortar. The formula is still the same by hand or machine: 1 part masonry mix cement (add lime if Portland cement) to 3 parts sand and the proper amount of water. You should make the mortar a bit stiffer than you use for bricks because it has to support about 20 pounds of weight. Incidentally, a mortar stand will save you so much effort while you work, and it's easy to put together. Just stand four blocks on end and put a 2′ × 3′ piece of ½-inch plywood on top of them. (It must be at least ½-inch plywood or it will bend under the weight.) Moisten the plywood before you put the mortar on it. Then throw 5 or 6 shovelsful on the stand — now you don't have to bend down so far.

Set Your First Block

Throw two rows of mortar on the footing — enough to lay the first block — and set it on the pencil mark. Your wall is 12 inches across and your block is 6 inches, so there will be 3 inches on either side. Position the block in the center but flush against the pencil mark. Level both ways. Then do the same at the other end. The purpose here is to set your mason's line. We use what's called a line stretcher, or you can lay a brick across the line to hold it, but whatever you use, it must be true. The line will assure you that the blocks are parallel and will be the line of the wall when laying the first course. However, you must double check the ends of the blocks with your level, both horizontal and vertical, to make sure they are true. The entire wall depends on those first two blocks.

Lay the First Course

First, apply a bed of mortar on the footing, about an inch thick and spread out enough to lay about three blocks. (Note the line stretcher in the photo.) You can't hold a block in your hand to butter it as you can with a brick, so stand them on end and apply mortar. Butter about an inch thick on both projections. You can do several at a time. Be generous with the mortar; a block is a lot of mass and you can scrape off the excess mortar and reuse it.

Before you lay your next block, butter the ends of the blocks already laid. Then place the block in the bed of mortar using your line as a guide. Tap it into place with your trowel handle until it is properly positioned. Put your short level across the block and check to see if it is level; adjust if needed. Continue until your last block is ready to be placed. This will be your "closure block" since your end block has already been laid. You might have a slight adjustment here to make this fit snugly. Try a dry fit first. If it looks about right, butter on both sides of the existing blocks (those already laid), then both sides of the closure block. This will allow it to slip into place smoothly. If it's a bit too loose, add more mortar.

To avoid surprises, use your measuring tape and check as you work; three blocks, including mortar, will measure 4 feet.

Corner

We built a return wall as a demonstration. Your wall may be straight. If so, ignore this step. It's simply a continuing of the first course at a 90 degree angle, including the end block and the closure block. However, you must take care to make your corner block plumb and level.

Start the Second Course

Lay off an amount of mortar on the outside edge of the block that has just been laid — both projections. Then lay off an equal amount on the inside edge of the block. You should probably mortar one block at a time until you get the hang of it, then you can spread ahead as shown in the photos. First lay your corner, level it and plumb to make true, then set your end block. This will be a half block at both ends of the second course so the joints will be staggered. The ends are set first, then the rest of the course so that you can make an adjustment in the wall if necessary, rather than at the end and wind up with a jagged edge.

You will need to set an additional standard size block alongside of the half block to provide added weight, otherwise the tension of your mortar line on your line stretcher will pull the half block loose. You now have an option to continue laying in this direction or start at the other end. A right-handed bricklayer would work left to right. As you lay the blocks, mortar will extrude out from the bottom and sides. Use the edge of your trowel to cut it off. After your first or second course is complete (your option), use your rat-tail jointer to finish off the joints — bottom and sides. This will provide a finished, concave look.

These photos show a 2-foot high wall. We placed the steel merely to show how it is installed. As mentioned, our codes are probably tougher than anywhere else in the country, to provide earthquake protection. However, you need steel to stand up to strong winds which occur everywhere.

We are obliged to use reinforcing steel horizontally in the footing and every two feet, which is every third course. It's important that you check the building codes in your area.

You can buy what are called channel blocks, which provide a groove on the bottom to fit over the steel and thus allow more mass of concrete around the steel for additional strength. However, don't use a channel block at the end because that would leave a hole in the wall and the mortar would leak out. Here you must notch one end of a standard block to accommodate the horizontal rebar. You can tap out a notch with a brick hammer. And since it's on the inside, no one will know if it's not neat.

When setting horizontal steel you should allow a 2-foot overlap where the steel ends and, obviously, don't go outside the wall. If there is a corner, make a 90 degree bend. This is easily done over your knee. A bricklayer will probably use bolt shears to cut rebar, but you can use a hacksaw to start the cut and then break off the end.

Verticals should be placed every 4 feet and bent under the horizontal steel in the footing. Where these occur, and after you have finished your first course, reach in and remove all excess mortar at the bottom of the cell, on top of the footing. You need your best bond at this point, so when you pour concrete (at the completion of the wall), it will fit tightly around the steel.

The Fourth Course

You can use standard blocks at the ends of this course. Set your end blocks, notched out, leveled, and plumbed. Repeat at the other end and set the line stretcher. This will be an entire channel course since you should accommodate the horizontal rebar.

NOTE: It might seem overkill to provide this kind of rebar support where there is no danger of earth-

quakes, but storm winds are an even greater threat. A broadside wind creates a vacuum on the lee side, so two forces act to increase the pressure on the wall. The ultimate authority, of course, is your own municipal building code.

Continue building until the wall reaches the desired height. On a 6-foot wall, lay the horizontal steel the next course from the top, i.e., one course below your last standard block course. This, then would also need channel blocks, except for the ends.

Pour Concrete

Your concrete should be a loose mixture of 1 part Portland cement, 3 parts sand, and 3 parts pea gravel. Pour all vertical steel cells. Where the horizontal overlap occurs, fill a 3-foot section of cells to provide added strength.

Cap It Off

A 2-inch thick cap block, the same color and material as your concrete blocks, will give the wall a finished look. It's best to use a cap that fits flush. You can buy larger sizes, but sometimes kids hang on these and break them off. It's your option.

SUMMARY

- Stake out wall and dig trench.
- Buy blocks, cement, sand, gravel. (Option: Rent mixer or order ready-mix.)
- Lay rebar and pour footing.
- Set end blocks and mason's line.
- Lay first course.
- Set half blocks at end of second course.
- Continue wall, setting horizontal rebar every two feet.
- Cap.

1. After the footing is poured and set, make a dry run.

2. Throw two rows of mortar on the footing and set the first block.

3. Butter an inch thick on both projections.

4. Apply mortar on both sides of the "closure" block. Make sure it fits snugly.

5. Apply enough mortar on the footing to lay about three blocks on your first course.

6. Verticals should be placed every 4 feet or third block (shown here 32" at corner).

7. The "closure" block is the last block in each course.

8. Start your second course with a half block. Use your level frequently to make sure blocks are true.

9. We place reinforcing steel every 2 feet or third course. The steel shown here is for demo purposes to show you how to bend the horizontal bar around the uprights. There should be 2 feet of overlap.

10. *Notch one end of a standard block to make a groove to fit over the horizontal steel. Use channel blocks with grooves in the bottom for the rest of the course.*

11. *Use a rat-tail jointer to make concave joints.*

12. *Brush off excess mortar to give the wall a neat, finished look.*

TUCKPOINTING

TOOLS & MATERIALS NEEDED

- [ ] Hammer
- [ ] Chisel
- [ ] Old paintbrush (1″ or 1½″)
- [ ] Sponge
- [ ] Tuckpointer
- [ ] Brick trowel or tuckpointing trowel
- [ ] Mixing container
- [ ] Mixing tools — hoe, shovel
- [ ] Safety glasses (should always be worn when working with brick or stone)
- [ ] Scaffolding
- [ ] Portland cement
- [ ] Sand
- [ ] Water
- [ ] Concrete glue (optional)
- [ ] Bag of mortar mix cement/sand (optional)

Tuckpointing is simply scratching out the old mortar from the joints of a brick or stone surface and filling in with new mortar. If you have a brick or stone home, or a wall surface of brick or stone veneer, you should look for cracks. These are caused by the building settling or, in the snowbelt, freezing moisture. Sometimes, with age, the mortar will crumble and the joints must be refilled. These cracks and the mortar deterioration will only get worse and costly water damage can easily occur, so you should get at them as soon as you can. Unless your walls are tumbling down, it's a relatively easy job. Here's how you do it.

Dig Out the Old

Use your hammer and chisel to dig out the old loose mortar. Be careful that you don't damage the bricks (or stone); you're just trying to remove the mortar.

Dig back to the hard mortar. The farther back you go, the harder it will be.

After you've dug out all the loose mortar, use an old paintbrush and clean out both the horizontal and vertical joints. Then dip the brush in water and remove the small grains so that you'll have a good bond with your fresh mortar. Apply water liberally. If your local hardware store carries *concrete glue* it's worth buying to ensure a better bond. Use a small paintbrush to paint the glue inside the joint, but don't get it on the face of the brick or stone; it will leave a shine when it dries.

Mix and Match

Sometimes it seems to me that everybody has his own idea about what proportion of sand and cement should be used to make the best mortar. (Almost like a favorite recipe for making Texas chili.) I use 3 parts sand to 1 part cement for our everyday jobs, but I recommend 2 parts sand to 1 part cement for this job. That's because you're using water in the joints and you're probably only working on a small area anyway. This richer mix will also dry faster.

As explained earlier, mortar should have the consistency of loose putty — or oatmeal, if you'd like (before you put in the milk). Add water sparingly. You can easily add more. But you'll have to add more sand and cement if your mortar is too soupy.

It is best to use #30 silica sand, but any clean sand will do. However, you are trying to *match* the existing mortar. When you're buying your sand and cement it's a good idea to ask the man at your hardware store or materials yard to help you with a cement color, if your existing mortar has an unusual shade or tint. Take a piece of loose material with you to show him. And the only way to make *sure* it matches is to make up a mortar sample.

Take your finger and put a swatch of mortar on a scrap brick or stone, and in a few seconds the edges will dry and show you how it will look. If you are matching a very light mortar, you might have to use a white cement with a white silica sand. Both are available at materials yards.

I don't mean to belabor the task of matching mortar. Close enough may be just fine with many homeowners, but you don't want your work to look like a patch job. (And, for what it's worth, if a professional tuckpointer is working on your home, it should be understood that the new mortar will match the old.)

How Much Mortar Will You Need to Mix?

If the job is a small one — and your first tuckpointing job probably is — you won't need more than a bucketful. And even more to the point, what should you mix it in? The best solution is a plastic tub or box. Discount stores such as K-Mart or Target sell them, often as kids' wading pools. You need one about 2 feet wide by 4 feet long and 8 to 12 inches deep. They are relatively inexpensive and easy to clean. You might also use a metal bed wheelbarrow. Most homeowners have one, as well as a hoe, to do the actual mixing. (After you finish, make sure you hose off the wheelbarrow bed thor-

oughly with clean water. Once cement mortar dries, it's difficult to remove.) Another alternative, since you probably only need a bucketful, is to use a plastic bucket for mixing your mortar. But whatever you use, be stingy adding water.

How much should you buy? Portland cement comes in paper sacks weighing 60, 80, or the standard one cubic foot size which weights 94 pounds. Your hardware store also sells sand in 60-pound sacks or larger, depending on where you live. That's probably a lot more than you need for a tuckpointing job. If you feel that you should keep these supplies on hand for future use, it's worth the modest purchase. If not, your hardware salesperson or materials yard operator probably has a broken bag in the back room and might sell you a small amount of cement. (It can't hurt to ask.)

There's another option that probably popped into your mind as we began this. Why not buy a bag of masonry mix, which is dry, already mixed sand/cement? You *can* do that, of course. And it's easier than mixing the proportions yourself. However, it's not as good because, in my professional opinion, there's not enough cement in the mixture. Also, it costs almost as much as the two separate bags of sand and cement that will net you more than double the amount of mortar. Believe me, that's a prime consideration for a professional mason.

It is extremely important to store dry cement properly, and to a lesser degree, sand as well. A good many homeowners store their bags in the garage or on the deck. Don't. If the floor gets wet, or moisture seeps up through the concrete floor, the bag will get wet and part of the cement will harden, which of course makes it useless. And then what do you do with it?

The best protection is to put the leftover cement and sand bags into a plastic trash bag. And even then, if you keep it in your garage, it's a good idea to put a piece of exterior-grade plywood under it.

Filling the Joints

Put some mortar in an old plastic bucket, and use the back of a brick trowel to hold the mortar while you fill the joints with a smaller trowel or your tuckpointer (see photo). The first thing you'll notice is that the mortar won't go in easily and you will slop mortar all over the face of the bricks. But that's all right because it will clean up easily after you're finished. And you'll drop more mortar than you can pack in the narrow joints. That's all right, too because you probably made a lot more than you thought you'd need. Soon you'll get the knack of it — probably by using your fingers to stuff the mortar in the cracks. (I do that, too. Whatever it takes.) Incidentally, if you do use your hands, kitchen sink rubber gloves are handy because the mortar sucks the moisture from your hands.

At this point, work on one brick at a time and fill the *bed* joint, or horizontal joint, first. When you have packed in as much mortar as you can, use your tuckpointer to press in and smooth it off. When it dries it should match the surrounding joints. (We'll get to concave joints later.) Then use a damp sponge to wipe off the face of the brick. Do the same with the *head* or vertical joints. Fill the crack with mortar, smooth it off with your tuckpointer, wipe off the excess mortar from the face of the brick with your damp sponge, and go on to fill the next joint. You'll need to go over and over each brick with your sponge to make sure it's clean. That's the way we do it, too. Once the mortar dries, that's the way it will look forever.

When your work dries you will notice a white powdery stain around your tuckpointed bricks. This should come off with a dry cloth unless you have been working with very hard brick. If so, use a cut-in-half sponge rubber ball, the kind kids play with. We always keep one in our tool box. Just rub the flat, dry surface over the brick and it will come clean.

Your tuckpointer tool will make a flat joint. If the surrounding joints are concave and you want your work to match, the tool to use is a rat-tail jointer. This is a rounded S-shaped tool that makes an indented joint.

Loose Stones

When a house settles, sometimes bricks or pieces of stone veneer can work loose or even fall out. If this problem affects no more than five or six pieces, the procedure for stone is as follows.

Lift out, or pry off, the loose stones and place them on the ground *in the same order* as they appeared on the siding. This is important because they might not fit properly if they are replaced out of order. Mix your mortar in the same 2 parts sand to 1 part cement proportions, but use a bit less water to get a drier mortar than you would use for bricks. Why? Because bricks will absorb moisture and stone veneer won't.

Before you start, paint cement glue around the joints surrounding your replacement pieces. Put some mortar on the surface in back and at the bottom of the replacement area. Then, starting from the bottom and going up, put mortar on the back and the bottom of the first piece and make a joint as each piece is replaced. Using your tuckpointer, do the horizontal joint first, then the vertical joints. Continue with each piece. Pack the last piece as tight as you can and hold it in place with your hand until it seems solid. Here again, you should match the color of your mortar as closely as you can so that it doesn't look like a patch job.

Cleaning Up

When you are finished, it's best to clean your equipment right away, not after lunch or later. When mortar dries and hardens on a tool or the bottom of your wheelbarrow, it's difficult to remove. Wash everything off with clean water and then dry it off. This includes your shoes if necessary. Since you might not be using your tools again for a while, it's a good idea to put a thin coating of oil on the surface of your trowel and tuck-pointer.

After you wash your hands you'll notice that the mortar has removed all the moisture from your palms. A couple of applications of hand cream will restore them to normal. (It's no fun holding hands with a bricklayer.)

SUMMARY

- Dig out the old mortar, clean out the joints with a dry brush.

- Mix mortar (2 parts sand, 1 part cement). Match to existing mortar.

- Apply with proper tool (tuckpointing trowel, jointer, fingers).

- Clean off with sponge and water. Wipe off white stain with a dry cloth or half of rubber ball.

- Clean up before mortar dries and hardens on tools.

- Use scaffolding when working above your reach.

RESTORING DETERIORATED BRICKS

TOOLS & MATERIALS NEEDED

☐ Tuckpointer
☐ Brick trowel
☐ Rubber gloves (optional)
☐ Mortar (Masonry mix okay)
☐ Cement color

Replace a Damaged Brick with a New One

Not too many years ago it was the custom in some parts of the country to use sandblasting to remove dirt and paint from the brick facade of old homes. It's not always wise to use this technique because many types of common brick have a hard surface and a soft interior. Sandblasting removes much of the hard surface and when the soft interior is exposed to the weather the brick starts to crumble. Today, cleaning bricks is often done with a chemical restoration process or with water, using a high pressure attachment. Both techniques are best left to a professional since there are potential dangers.

The proper procedure to repair deteriorated bricks or a brick surface which has crumbled is to replace the damaged brick with good used brick. It should match the surrounding bricks as closely as possible.

Use a hammer and chisel to cut out the damaged brick. Take care not to cut or damage the adjacent bricks. Then wet down the open area with a paintbrush and water. Next, apply mortar to the replacement brick and make your joints. Pack in your mortar with a small tuckpointing trowel (and your fingers, if necessary), and use a tuckpointer to match the adjacent joints. When you mix your mortar try to match the existing joints as closely as possible.

Construct your Own Brick

Sometimes it's not possible to dig out a damaged brick to replace it with a good one. In this situation, you can rebuild the damaged brick with matching colored mortar. This is the procedure we followed to repair a one-course chimney in a century-old home in Galena, Illinois. Replacing the bricks might have weakened the structure and caused the chimney to fall.

1. Clean out the crumbled brick with a hammer and chisel. You might also use a large screwdriver. The decayed brick comes out easily. A dry paintbrush will remove the small particles.

2. Wet down the area thoroughly. You can use a garden hose set at low pressure. Brick absorbs water like a sponge, so unless your work area is damp, the bricks will remove the water from your mortar. This will cause the mortar to dry too fast and to crumble.

3. Mix the mortar. We didn't have many bricks to repair so we used an old paint bucket for a mixing container. For a small job, part of a bag of masonry mix works fine if you add about 25% Portland cement to get a richer mix. Then add a small amount of red cement color. This is a dry, powdery substance that looks like colored flour and comes in a variety of earth tones. A little goes a long way. You can buy cement color in a construction materials or hardware store, or if all else fails, from a ready-mix plant.

Cover entire area, joints and all, and cut in outline of brick with tuckpointer.

Use back of trowel to hold mortar and use tuckpointer to make the joints.

When your mortar color looks right, make a test smear on the corner of a brick to see how it will look when it dries. If you're slightly off, adjust your mix accordingly but use the color sparingly.

When your mortar is ready, gently hose down the work area again.

4. Apply the mortar. Use a small tuckpointing trowel to make the joints. If you also have a larger brick trowel, you can use the back of it to hold the mortar close to the job while you pack the cavity of the damaged brick. Cover the entire area flush with the adjacent bricks, joints and all. There is no need to be neat because you will clean off the excess.

If you have several bricks to replace, continue the procedure until all are filled.

5. Wet a sponge — the kind you use for washing your car will work fine — and with a light, rotating movement, smooth out the new mortar. Then let it set for about five minutes.

Next, with your tuckpointer, start cutting out a joint around your new brick. You can use a small board as a guide to keep your line straight. Cut out all four sides of each brick, about ½″ deep, just a bit lower than the surrounding joints. Cut the top first, then the sides, and finally the bottom joint. You are thus literally building a brick out of matching mortar.

6. Mix more mortar, but this time don't use color; try to match the existing joints. Fill in the joints around your newly constructed brick to match the existing mortar. Use your tuckpointer to overlap the adjacent joints. You might find it easier to use your fingers to pack in the head (vertical) joints. Another technique is to hold a ball of mortar in one hand while you use your tuckpointer or your fingers to pack in the joint. You will find it easier on your hands if you use rubber gloves. The kind used for washing dishes works fine.

7. Wet your sponge and remove the excess mortar. This will take repeated wipings, so use first one side then the other. Then rinse and repeat the operation as many times as it takes to make your work absolutely clean. It must be clean because once it dries, that's the way it will look forever. After each brick has been cleaned, if you can set your hose on low spray, *very gently* spray your work area to keep the mortar from drying too fast. This is especially important if you have been working in direct sun.

8. Finally, clean your tools. Wash the mortar off now, or you won't get it off later.

SUMMARY

- If possible, replace damaged brick with new one — match mortar.
- If not possible, cut away damaged portion of brick.
- Wet down area.
- Use cement color to make mortar that matches bricks and "make" brick from mortar.
- Cut in joints.
- Use regular mortar to make joints on new "bricks."
- Clean area with sponge.
- Spray gently.

DRY BRICK WALK

A brick walk can add a great deal of charm to your yard. The materials are relatively inexpensive and it's not that difficult to build, especially if you break it down to a one-step-at-a-time operation. Since it's a dry walk, you have no mortar to mix or joints to make.

Measure the Walk

Using a tape measure, a mason's line, and a number of wood stakes, block out the dimensions of your walk. It's important to get the exact width because your bricks must fit snugly together within the confines of your edging.

The best way to make sure the bricks fit is to make a dry run with a single course in width. You will also have to determine the type of bond you want to use. The two easiest bonds, or patterns, to work with are the Basket Bond and the Running Bond (see illustration).

For our purposes, let's assume you want to use the Basket Bond. Lay out a test course on top of the dirt (or lawn) and allow for the width of your 2″ × 4″ edging. Then set your stakes and tie on your lines on each side of your walk site.

TYPES OF BONDS

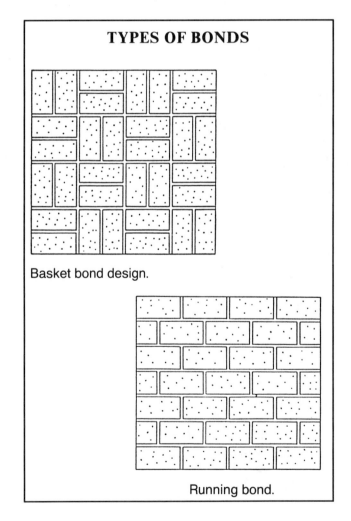

Basket bond design.

Running bond.

Remove Soil

You will need to remove about 7 inches of soil. The bricks measure 3 inches and you will need 2 or 3 inches of sand for a bed. The depth may wary; for example, if you are removing sod you should have the tops of your brick even with the lawn on either side of the walk.

If your path runs alongside the house, you should slope your excavation so that the rain will run off away from the house. It can be a gentle slant of about ½ inch on a 3-foot wide walkway. If the path runs toward the house, make certain that there is a drain that will deflect the runoff.

Set the Edging

Use treated (Wolmanized) lumber for your 2″ × 4″ edgings and stakes because these will be placed in the dirt and you want to retard decay. Redwood can also be used if treated wood is not available. Buy as many lengths as you need for both sides and ends of the walk. Securely staked edging is a must to keep the bricks in your path contained so they don't "walk away."

Set the inside of your first piece of edging under your line and set your stake, driving it securely into the dirt. The stake should be driven on the outside and the edging nailed to the stake. The inside must be clear so that the bricks fit without cutting. Make sure the width is constant for the entire length of the walk. Do one side at a time and set a stake about every three feet.

Next build a screed (see illustration) from 1″ × 6″ lumber. This is a device that will allow you to scrape off the proper amount of sand so that your bricks will lie evenly. You should make the cutout portion ¼ inch less than the height of the brick so that you can place it firmly in the sand.

For protection against freezing (if that's a problem in your area) and weeds (they are always a problem), put down a layer of plastic sheeting before you add your sand.

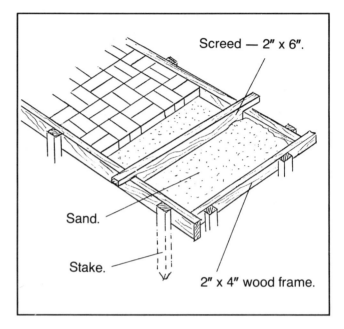

Screed — 2″ x 6″.

Sand.

Stake.

2″ x 4″ wood frame.

Dump in Sand and Lay Bricks

You should buy enough sand to come up to the tops of the edging. About a half ton of sand should be sufficient for a walkway measuring 3′ × 18′ × 3″ deep. To make sure, consult with your materials yard salesperson and tell him the dimensions of your walk.

Before you begin, you'll need your screed and a foot long piece of 2″ × 4″ to use as a tamp. Place your screed inside the edging at the beginning of the staked out path, kneel down behind it in the sand, and pull it toward you. Don't work more than 2 or 2½ feet at a time. You will notice the section of sand you have screeded is still loose, so take the length of 2″ × 4″ and tap the surface gently to compact it. If the surface is too low, sprinkle some more sand and if need be, screed again. It's not absolutely necessary, but you might consider sprinkling water on the finished area of sand to make it more firm as you lay your bricks. (After you lay a few courses you'll get the feel of it and develop your own touches.)

Now lay your first course of bricks, using the basket bond — two bricks with the path, two across; then reverse the pattern for the next course (see illustration). Lay the bricks on the sand; at this time they should be ¼ inch above the frame. As you lay your pattern (see illustration) make sure that your bricks are snug and tight against each other and that each brick is level. You will notice that the basket bond is a fraction wider than it is long, so one course is tight and the other is ¼ inch loose. That's no problem.

If you are working alone, it will help to place bricks at intervals along the outsides of the walk so that you can reach them without getting up. Once you get into the rhythm, the path will grow fast.

At the end, you might have to cut bricks to fit spaces, and the easiest way to do this is to purchase a masonry cutting blade for your hand power saw. This costs under $3 and is worth the money because it makes cutting easy and accurate. It is a dusty job, however, so you should wear a painter's mask and certainly your safety glasses.

An alternative for cutting bricks is to use a 5-inch brick set and a mason's hammer. After you mark the line of your cut, place the set (chisel) on the mark and strike sharply. You can cut bricks best in the loose sand and, with a little practice, you can hold the set at an angle to cut the brick so it will fit snugly in an existing space.

Work your way down the path until you reach the end piece of edging. When the entire path has been laid, if your bricks have been laid level, they are ¼ inch above the edging. To make them level with the edging and to make sure they won't shift, take your small 2″ × 4″ tamp and tap lightly on each brick with your hammer until it drops ¼ inch. Don't walk on your work yet. Do the tamping from either side and reach in toward the center.

After your bricks are all firm and level, throw loose dry sand over your bricks to fill in the joints. You can use the shovel to scatter the sand. Then use a push broom to sweep the sand into the small cracks. Use a criss-cross motion to make sure every crevice is filled so you lock the bricks firmly in place.

When this is done you can walk on your path. Don't remove the edging.

Back Fill and Enjoy Your Work

Fill in the dirt along the outside of your edging and sweep off the path. Then have a cool drink and enjoy your handiwork.

SUMMARY

- Determine dimensions of your path.
- Dig away about 7 inches of soil.
- Set edging: nail 2″ × 4″ lengths securely inside wood stakes. Include edging at each end of the path. Use treated lumber.
- Put in layer of plastic sheeting and dump in sand.
- Screed sand and lay bricks in basket bond. Tamp gently after finish.
- Spread sand on top of path and sweep.
- Back fill sides of path.

CONCRETE BLOCK GARDEN WALL

TOOLS & MATERIALS NEEDED

- ☐ 2-hole concrete blocks (if not available, use 3-hole blocks)
- ☐ Sand, gravel, cement — for concrete and mortar
- ☐ 2″ × 4″ lengths of lumber
- ☐ 2-foot wood stakes
- ☐ Rebar (reinforcing steel) ⅜ inch diameter
- ☐ Tie wire
- ☐ Mixer
- ☐ Pick and shovel
- ☐ Pliers
- ☐ Hammer and nails
- ☐ Trowel
- ☐ Jointer
- ☐ Brick hammer
- ☐ Torpedo level and 3-foot mason's level
- ☐ Mason's line
- ☐ Pipe for bending rebar

For a 20-foot wall, 6 feet high:

- ☐ 15 blocks for each of 9 courses = 135 blocks plus 9 half blocks
- ☐ 2 20-foot lengths of rebar
- ☐ 11 uprights × 2 drop-ins = 22 4-foot pieces
- ☐ 15 cap blocks

Before You Begin

NOTE: See Building a Concrete Block Wall for further information on laying concrete blocks.

For garden walls I use a 6″ wide × 8″ high × 16″ long 2-hole block. The instructions that follow are based on this type of block. The 2-hole block is the most commonly used in California because it provides a greater concrete mass around the reinforcing steel. If you use a 3-hole block make sure you set your steel so that it fits in the center hole.

We frequently build concrete block garden walls to replace the existing redwood fences that separate the backyard property on three sides of a house and provide the necessary privacy that most Californians demand. I should point out that land costs in southern California are so high that lots are generally narrow and houses are close to each other. In Los Angeles County a lot must contain 5000 square feet, and a typical lot measures 50 feet wide and 100 feet deep.

Since the fence usually rests on the property line, the homeowners on either side of the fence are traditionally responsible for upkeep. It doesn't always work out that way because while you might paint and tend your side of the fence, your next door neighbor could be unconcerned about its maintenance, which leads inevitably to deterioration and eventual replacement. Concrete block walls are virtually indestructible and require no maintenance.

Because the wall is a shared project we observe these procedures:

- We advise the neighbor of our intention to replace the existing fence with a new concrete block wall. The neighbor's permission is necessary before the fence can be removed.

- We make certain that the wall is exactly on the property line, especially since the wall is 6 inches wide; usually a couple inches wider than a fence which uses 4' × 4" upright posts and 1-inch redwood boards.

- We invite the neighbor to pay half, or part, of the cost if he or she would like. If building the wall is a joint venture, there is no problem, but if it is a complete surprise the neighbor may have some natural reluctance to contribute to someone else's project, even though he might benefit from it.

- If the neighbor wants to retain the wood fence, it's still possible to build a block wall provided it is entirely on our customer's property, although this is a rare occurrence.

Dig a Trench

Before you do anything, measure the existing fence. You'll need that figure to determine how many blocks to buy. Then put stakes at each end of the fence and remove it. Set up your mason's line exactly on the center of the property line and dig a trench 12 inches deep and 12 to 14 inches wide. If your land is on a slight incline, cut steps, with increments of 4 inches. This is because you can buy blocks that are 4 inches high, and these will keep your courses level when you start to lay blocks. Use your mason's or carpenter's level to make sure that your mason's line is level.

Set 2" × 4" Horizontal Support

The bottom of the 2" × 4" support should be level with, or slightly below, the top of your existing soil. It should be secured with stakes and set down the center of the trench. Use as many lengths of 2" × 4" as you need. (If you have to join two 2" × 4"s together, butt the two ends together and nail on a 1" × 4" splint on the outside.) Stake it on one side only, every 6 to 8 feet. The stakes must be at least two feet long to provide proper support. The starting edge of your 2" × 4" should be fixed so that it will also be the starting edge of your first block.

The walls of the trench are the actual form for your poured concrete footing.

Place Rebar

You'll need a piece of ⅜ inch rebar, or reinforcing steel, at the bottom of your trench to secure the footing. But you can't just drop the rebar on the dirt at the bottom of the trench or it will rust away, so the easiest way is to lay the rebar on special 3" × 3" concrete blocks or spacers. They're designed for this job and they have a little piece of wire to secure the rebar. Use as many pieces as needed and secure the overlaps with wire. (You should have a 2-foot overlap.) Rebar comes in 20-foot lengths, but you can also buy it in a variety of shorter lengths. You should have the rebar delivered with your concrete blocks.

If you don't use these 3 inch blocks, you can also set wood stakes down the center and secure the rebar to the stakes with small pieces of wire. However, you must keep the rebar 3 inches off the ground and clear of the dirt or it will rust.

Set Vertical Rebar

The vertical rebar should be the same ⅜ inch reinforcing steel that you used for your horizontal, but cut in 4-foot lengths. Starting with the first hole in your first concrete block, you should place a rebar upright in the middle of the hole, 24 inches apart, along your trench. NOTE: This is based on using 2-hole blocks.

The rebar provides the necessary strength to your concrete cores in the event of strong winds. An unsupported garden wall can catch the wind like a sail. As a licensed contractor, I guarantee anything I put on any property. If anything happens, I must tear it all out and start over again. It's obviously worth my while to do it right the first time. The same holds true for a homeowner. When you install a wall, you won't want to do it again in your lifetime. You might be tempted to forget the rebar uprights, but it's a worthwhile procedure, even in a sheltered area.

You must secure the rebar so that it stays in place until you pour your footing. Take a piece of ordinary pipe, about an inch in diameter and insert the end of your 4-foot piece of rebar about 4 inches. Then bend the rebar to make an "L" shape. You'll find it bends easily. Next, hook the "L" under the horizontal, Then secure it with a piece of wire.

Secure the upright to the 2″ × 4″ support just at the top of your trench. You can put a nail on either side of the rebar and then wire it so it stays erect. Your first rebar vertical should be set exactly 4 inches from the edge of the 2″ × 4″ support. This will place the vertical rebar exactly in the center of the first hole in your first concrete block. Make a dry test to make sure that it is. When you are certain your measurements are correct, set a vertical rebar every 24 inches along your trench. It's important to place the rebar verticals properly because when you start laying block, after your footing is poured, you'll have to lift the block over the top of the rebar, and it obviously must fit the block. If you must use less than 3 feet, use increments of 8 inches so you can match the holes in the blocks. You might have to do this for your last horizontal.

Pour the Footing

You are now ready to pour your concrete footing. This will fill in the trench, encasing your horizontal rebar and your vertical rebar supports. Fill to the bottom of your 2″ × 4″ at the top of your trench. Depending on the depth of your trench, this footing will be about 12 inches high. Don't cement in the 2″ × 4″. That must be removed after the footing has set.

You will need one cubic yard of concrete for every 25 feet of wall. Our 100-foot wall would therefore take 4 cubic yards of concrete. (One cubic yard equals 27 cubic feet, but you should allow for some waste and the fact that your trench might be wider or deeper than you had planned.)

If you rent a power mixer and mix it yourself, the proportions should be 1 part Portland cement, 3 parts sand, and 3 parts gravel. For a wall 20 feet long, this would be about 6 sacks of Portland cement, ¾ ton of sand, and 2 tons of pea gravel.

You can also get prices from a ready-mix concrete company and compare costs. You'll need to provide dimensions and they'll figure the rest. Since a ready-mix truck must have close access to your site, you might also ask about a concrete pump.

After the footing has been poured, let it set overnight and the next day remove the 2″ × 4″ support and the uprights will be firmly embedded. Then clean off the footing with a broom. NOTE: It's worth your while to clean off the 2″ × 4″s so you can use them again. I nail them together temporarily so they don't bow.

Lay Blocks

First, mix a batch of mortar. As we mentioned elsewhere, don't make more than you can use in an hour, or less. Start with one bag of cement and see how it goes. Make a 3-to-1 mix — 3 parts sand to 1 part cement. Mix it a bit stiff because it has to support the weight of a concrete block weighing 18 to 20 pounds. (There are approximately 7 shovelsful of cement in a standard 94-pound sack, so I use about 24 shovelsful of sand. You might keep this in mind if you are buying sand by the ton.)

The procedure for laying concrete blocks is as follows. Spread a bed of mortar on the footing — 1 inch thick and 2 or 3 blocks long. Then stand the block on end and trowel on mortar, an inch thick on both projections at the end of the block. Put pressure on the block to get a ⅜ inch joint. Use a torpedo level across the top — both ways — to make sure the block is level. Before you butter your next block, put mortar on the end of the block, and repeat the action.

Place your first block over the rebar upright in mortar as indicated. Make sure it's level and then

Vertical rebar supports are placed 48 inches apart — every third block.

This section of the wall is tied into a standing wall and uses an existing chain link fence post as added support. (It's also easier to build around the post than to cut it off and fill in the hole.) Note the channel block for horizontal rebar.

Completed wall is 9 courses high . . . 6 feet plus the cap.

lay a temporary block at the far end of the wall. Then drive stakes at each end, past the footing, and tie on a mason's line so it just touches the back corner of each block. Then use this to set the rest of the blocks in the first course.

You must remove the excess mortar and tool the joints — both the bed (bottom) and the head (side) joints — with a rat-tail jointer, and on both sides of the wall. (Even if your neighbor isn't paying his share.)

When you get to the end of the first course, you might have to adjust, or remove, the temporary block to fit the wall. Before you start your second course, use your hand to remove the excess mortar in every cell that has a vertical rebar. You will pour concrete in these cells later.

On the second course, you'll need a half block at each end. You can buy this size. For a 6-foot high wall, you'll need 8 to 10 half blocks, one at each end of every other course.

When you start your second course, spread mortar on top of the first block in your first course and place on the half block. Level both ways with a torpedo level. Then set a half block at the other end and set your mason's line as you did before. You will have to drop your blocks over the rebar uprights on each of your courses, at least until the wall becomes higher than the rebar uprights.

As you complete each course, clean off the excess mortar and use a rat-tail jointer to make joints. Do this on both sides of the wall.

Your ninth course should put you at the standard 6-foot height; however, for this course you use a slightly different block. It's called a channel block because it has a notch to receive a horizontal bar of reinforcing steel. The rebar should run the full length of this top course of the wall. Where you must join two pieces of rebar, overlap a 2-foot section and wrap with wire. At the ends use a regular block and cut a notch in the web and inside

end. The outside end should be solid so the rebar is not exposed to rust.

Mix Concrete for Grouting Cells

You'll need to pour this batch of concrete, so make it a bit thinner than your footing concrete but use the same proportions (1 part cement, 3 parts sand, 3 parts pea gravel). It's easiest to pour from a bucket and you should fill each of the cells where you used the rebar uprights. Fill them level with the top of the block. When the concrete has become stiff, but not too hard, place a 4-foot section of rebar in each of these cells. This will overlap the embedded upright and provide full 6-foot steel reinforcement. Insert the bar slightly lower than the top of the block. (The wall is 6 feet high and your vertical rebar uprights are 4 feet high, so you need an additional 4-foot length of $\frac{3}{8}$-inch rebar which will give you a 2-foot overlap for added strength at every reinforced cell.)

Cap the Wall

The final step is to put on a course of caps, which measure 6 inches wide, 2 inches high, and 16 inches long. These are laid just like block and there is no cutting needed. However, you should remove the excess mortar and make the joints on this course as well, including your neighbor's side. You can buy caps in a variety of colors such as brown, tan, or pink.

When your concrete has set, clean up and enjoy your wall. It should last the life of your house.

SUMMARY

- Measure line and set mason's line. Then remove existing fence.

- Dig trench 12 inches deep and 12 to 14 inches wide. If land slopes, cut steps at 4-inch increments. Use 4-inch high blocks to level off.

- Set 2″ × 4″ stud horizontal support down the center of the trench; the bottom of the stud should be level with the top of your soil. Secure with 2-foot stakes.
- Place 3″ × 3″ blocks at the bottom of the trench.
- Lay horizontal ⅜-inch rebar the length of the trench on top of these blocks (to keep the steel off the dirt). Secure with wire affixed to the blocks.
- Set vertical 4-foot lengths of rebar every 32 inches. Place 4 inches in from the start mark. Secure to horizontal rebar at bottom of the trench and, to keep upright, also to the horizontal 2″ × 4″ stud.
- Mix concrete and pour footing up to bottom of 2″ × 4″ support. Remove support after drying time.
- Mix mortar and lay block. Use a half block at ends, starting with second course and for every other course to stagger joints. Remove excess mortar and tool joints with rat-tail jointer or tuckpointing tool. Drop blocks over upright rebars.
- Use channel blocks for top (ninth) course and set horizontal rebar. Cut notches in end blocks to fit rebar.
- Mix concrete and pour (from bucket) into cells with rebar. Fill to level of top block. Before the concrete starts to set insert 4-foot lengths of rebar alongside upright steel supports. Push in to slightly below top of concrete.
- Set caps on top course and clean up.

REPLACING AN EXISTING BLACKTOP DRIVEWAY WITH A NEW CONCRETE DRIVEWAY

TOOLS & MATERIALS NEEDED

- ☐ Pickax
- ☐ Wrecking bar
- ☐ Front end loader (possibly)
- ☐ Lengths of 2″ × 4″
- ☐ Lengths of redwood benders
- ☐ 12-inch or 16-inch stakes
- ☐ Hammer and nails
- ☐ Drainage tile or PVC plastic pipe sections (possibly)
- ☐ Sand
- ☐ Ready-mix concrete

If you have an older home (in Southern California forty years easily qualifies), your blacktop asphalt driveway might be due for replacement. It could be buckling because adjacent trees have pushed an expanding root system under the blacktop, or breaking up from upheavals caused by frost, or deteriorating from leaking crankcase oil, or a combination of the above.

It's a fairly big job and you will need help to replace your existing blacktop driveway with a new concrete driveway, but you can do much of the work yourself and save almost half of the cost. I just did such a job for my daughter (near Pasadena, CA) on a very tight budget. Here's how you can do it.

Just one reminder before we start. Since you are replacing an existing driveway, you should have no problem with city hall but, depending on your locality, you might have to take out a construction permit and pay a nominal fee. You should check the appropriate department that handles such work at your local government. It's conceivable that the work might also be subject to inspection.

Remove the Old Blacktop

You'll find that the blacktop will break off in pieces when you use a large wrecking bar or a pickax to pry under and lift up. If you have a relatively small area you can do it by hand without any great effort. A large driveway might require the use of a small front-end loader or grader. CAUTION: If you do use heavy equipment, make sure you don't cut into any existing water or gas lines. Generally, however, the problem is not removing the blacktop, it's getting rid of it when you're through.

Many asphalt paving companies will accept your broken pieces of blacktop which they will crush and reuse. They certainly won't pay you for it, and you'll have to cart it out to them, but at least you won't have to pay a dump fee. You might call a paving company in your area to make sure. In any event, don't start tearing up your driveway before you have a means to dispose of the rubble. And if you don't have a pickup truck, or can't borrow one, you might consider renting a trailer. On my job, I threw the broken pieces of blacktop right into my truck to avoid rehandling and drove the load out to the nearest asphalt plant and dumped it — with their permission, of course.

Grade the Driveway

After all of the broken asphalt and rubble have been removed, grade the driveway down to 5 or 5½ inches below the garage door. Your original black-top probably was at least 4 inches so you shouldn't have a monumental grading job, unless you have an enormous driveway. Start at the door and work out to the street. If you have a sidewalk in front of your house, you can only go to the sidewalk, which usually belongs to the city.

Drainage is obviously a prime consideration, but presumably your original blacktop driveway had already resolved that problem. If your driveway was above the street, the water drained away from the house, down the drive, and into the gutter of the street. Your new drive should do the same. If your drive is below the street level, you want the water to course off the side (or sides) and into a drain, or whatever solves your problem, but certainly not back toward the house.

If you have always had a drainage problem, now's the time to resolve it. You can do this with drainage tile or sections of PVC pipe to carry the water away. Just make sure the water doesn't drain back toward your house . . . or your neighbor's house. While you're at it, you could also tie in your downspout drains from the roof into the system. You can buy connecting links to join downspouts, 3- or 4-inch corrugated tile, or lengths of plastic pipe.

Set Your Forms

After you have finished grading, set the forms which will hold the poured concrete in place until it dries. Use 2″ × 4″s for the straight sections and redwood "benders" if you have a turning circle or a curving section. Usually a bender is a ½″ thick board and 4 inches wide. They often come in 20-foot sections, and you nail them together to get as big a circle or arc as you need.

Nail your 2″ × 4″s or benders to 12- or 16-inch stakes. The ground was extremely hard on my job so I had to use 16-inch stakes for the necessary support. It is important to make the forms rigid so the concrete won't push the stakes (and forms) out

of position. *Make sure you nail the stakes on the outside of the forms.*

It's my belief that a concrete driveway adds a note of class and distinction to a home. When it's put in properly, it will last forever, but there's no guarantee it won't crack. So here's what I do to help the situation and to give a custom look to the drive-way. Every 10 to 12 feet I put in a strip of brick to allow for expansion and to help reduce the chances of cracking. It's not that difficult because you put the brick in after the concrete has been poured and hardened.

To make a space for the bricks, position two lengths of 2″ × 4″, on their sides, facing each other. They must be the full width of the driveway. Then cut off three 6-inch pieces of 2″ × 4″ and put these — as stretchers — between the two lengths of 2″ × 4″; one in the center, one at each end. Set up these 2″ × 4″ strips every 10 to 12 feet or however it apportions out for the length of your drive.

IMPORTANT: Because of the wear, traffic, and danger of frost, you should use a hard-face brick for your separator strips, maybe even a paver. So it's imperative that you have the bricks on hand before you build your separator forms to make sure that they will fit the form.

This gives you a 9-inch opening. When you remove the strip after the concrete has hardened you will have enough room for an 8-inch brick plus a half-inch mortar joint on either side. You must stake these forms on the *inside* so when you pull out the forms you have a straight line of concrete.

Add a Bed of Sand

To cut cost somewhat, I didn't want to pour a full 5½ inches of concrete so I put in a 2-inch bed of sand. This is also a good safety protection for snowbelt areas. (If you need a deeper bed of sand for severe freezing conditions, grade deeper before putting in your forms. Check with your local authorities. However, you will need not less than 3½ inches of concrete.) This driveway, with 3½ inches of poured concrete, probably wouldn't stand up under sustained semi-truck traffic, but it will be plenty strong enough for your home traffic, even if you have teenagers.

Get a Finisher

Make one last check to be sure your forms are in, securely fastened (with stakes on the outside), and the sand bed has been evened out.

Except for one more action, you have probably gone as far as you can. From this point on you need help. I did, too. What you *can* do first, is to measure the drive — the width, length, and depth. Write down the figures, then call the ready-mix company in your area and ask for a professional finisher to handle the job from this point on. You can't do this yourself, and you'd be foolish to try.

Most of the ready-mix concrete companies have such people, either on staff, or they know of independent specialists who work on custom jobs. You'll want a finisher to come out to your site and inspect your job to make certain it meets his specifications before he starts to work. If he feels your work should be improved, chances are he'll tell you how to do it. He will also double check your figures and tell you how much concrete you'll need. Then after you agree on his fee and the cost of the concrete you'll need, check on availabilities.

I have my own procedure for working with ready-mix concrete companies which I'll pass along for what it's worth. First, depending on the amount of construction work in your area, they're usually busy. I always try to get the first load in the morning — that's about 7 a.m. in our area. After that, it might be difficult to pin down a time. Depending on the restrictions in your area, the trucks are limited to the amount of load they can carry (because of the over-the-road weight). In our part of the country it's 9½ yards, which, together with the

truck itself, is about 26 tons. You should also put in your order several days in advance.

There's another thing that you should talk over with the finisher, and that's where the mixing truck will park to dump your concrete. The driver sure can't use your driveway. Chances are you have a lawn, garden, trees, or some kind of landscaping that you don't want crushed. If the truck can get fairly close to the site they might be able to use the sections of troughs that come with the truck. These will direct the flow of concrete exactly where the finisher wants it. If not, you'll need a concrete pump that handles the flow through a hose. Make sure the ready-mix company knows that you'll need one. It's not always standard equipment.

It will also cost additionally for labor, but it sure beats — heaven forbid — using a mason's wheelbarrow, and shlepping it on. That would take forever and would certainly run up the cost of the concrete because of the time involved.

Every finisher is different. Some like help, some don't. Chances are he'll have his own equipment — especially screeds — for smoothing out and leveling off the concrete as it's poured into your forms. If your finisher doesn't have his screeds, you might build them for him out of 2″ × 4″s. He can tell you what he needs.

When the concrete is poured and is in the process of hardening, it is traditionally watered — like your lawn — to slow down the drying and prevent cracking. Use the finest spray, more like a mist, if you can keep it that fine. This is done over a period of several days, every few hours if it's hot. But there's a much better way, called the Hunt's Process. It's actually a wax that is sprayed from a portable air pressure sprayer. This seals the concrete so the moisture can't get out, and the drying process is slowed down. The slower it dries, the stronger it will be. It costs a little extra, but it's worth it. When the Hunt's Process is used you don't water because you would then wash off the wax. Ask about it.

Use 2" x 4" pieces for the straight sections and redwood benders for the curved parts (see foreground).

Stake the separators on the inside because these will be removed after the concrete has set. Separator space will be filled with bricks.

Brick separators will reduce the chances of the concrete cracking.

When concrete is set, remove first the stretchers between the separators,
then the stakes, then the 2" x 4"s before laying brick.

Remove the Forms

After a couple of days, the concrete will be dry enough to remove the forms. Take them out gently to avoid chipping the concrete. You can walk on the driveway but don't drive your car on it yet. You probably paid between $40 and $50 for the 2″ × 4″s. Once you clean off the concrete, they're perfectly good, so it's worthwhile to store them for future sue. They will bow, however, so here's an easy way to keep that from happening. Stack them by twos, one on top of the other, then nail them together. Then nail a third, then a fourth. Don't stack more than four in a block because they'll be too heavy to lift.

Before you remove the 2″ × 4″s running across the driveway as your brick separators, use a hammer to knock out the 6-inch stretchers between the 2″ × 4″s. Don't try to remove the separators as a unit. First, take out the 6-inch stretchers, then take out the stakes, then the 2″ × 4″s. Next, with a small shovel (your opening is only 9 inches wide), or a garden trowel or hoe, remove the dirt between the concrete sections. Don't chip the concrete. Dig down about 7 or 8 inches from the surface of the newly poured driveway and level it off.

Set the Bricks

First, mix up a small batch of concrete for a bed to lay the bricks on. You can use the standard proportion of 1 part cement, 3 parts sand, and 3 parts pea gravel. Mix it a bit stiff so it doesn't run.

Then, from a 12- to 14-inch section of 2″ × 6″ board, make a small screed to fit in the 9-inch space between the two sections of driveway (see illustration). Cut it ¼ inch less in depth than the brick. (When you push the brick into the concrete bed you'll make up this ¼ inch.)

Pour an amount of concrete into the opening and level it off with your screed. Then lay your first brick and tap it gently into the concrete bed until it's level with the top of your driveway. Next, lay your second brick, allowing a finger's width for the mortar joint between the bricks. (Don't worry about the joints at this point.) Continue across the driveway, adding more concrete for your bed as you need it, screeding to get the proper depth. Do a 6-foot section at a time.

When you have filled in the complete width, mix a small batch of mortar to grout between the bricks. Here use 1 part cement and 3 parts sand. Mix it a bit stiff to avoid staining the bricks.

This means that you'll have to use your brick trowel to work the mortar between the bricks. You can also use a tuckpointer to help work the mortar in so you don't leave any air spaces. Then use this (or a rat-tail jointer) to make a concave joint between the bricks and at each end against the driveway sections.

When all of the bricks are set in your first section, get a damp sponge and a bucket of water and clean off the excess mortar. You may have to go over and over to get the bricks clean, and you might also use a half of a sponge rubber ball for rubbing. The trick is to keep the bricks dry at this point and they will come clean.

Continue for as many strips as you have allowed and wait at least three days for the bricks to set before driving a car on your new driveway. Then fill in the dirt alongside the driveway and you're set for the life of the house.

Options

REPLACE PIPES

When the blacktop was removed we anticipated future water line problems and decided to replace the existing line. Now this is southern California with no severe freezing problems, so the water lines were close to the surface. If you live in the northern part of the country these would be buried several feet deep. In any event, at least one of the three lines that I put in is applicable to you wherever you live.

The house, built some twenty-five years ago, had a galvanized water main, which doesn't usually last too long. And I certainly didn't want to use a concrete saw at some future date to cut across our new driveway to fix a leaky water line. So I replaced it with 1-inch copper: three lengths, soldered together, hooked up, and buried about 24 inches deep. (We have no freeze-up problems.) I'm not a plumber, but it's not all that difficult a job.

Next I installed an underground sprinkler line and hooked it up to the faucet by the front door. I used ¾-inch plastic pipe (PVC) for this and buried it 12 inches deep. You can buy all sorts of connecting links. And finally I laid a 3-inch plastic pipe buried 8 inches deep under the width of the driveway just in case anyone has to snake something through it. Who knows what or when? I also marked where the outlets can be found. (Someday someone will bless me for my ounce of prevention.)

NOTE: If you install any underground pipes, you should do this work before you put in the forms.

COLOR

If you are tempted to have your concrete tinted a soft pink or earth shade, I would advise against it for these reasons. Some colors are quite expensive, and you pay by the yard. But more than that, the colors rarely stay uniform, especially on a driveway. If one area is more exposed to the sun it will turn a different shade than a section of concrete shaded by a tree.

Cost

Size: Approximately 1200 square feet of driveway to cover. This is a cost breakdown.

Concrete: About 14 cubic yards	$ 840.00
Finisher	200.00
Concrete pump	95.00
Lumber	40.00
Hunt's Process Sealer	25.00
Total	$1200.00
Job bid	$2200.00
Cost of job (above)	1200.00
Saving to homeowner	1000.00

SUMMARY

- Remove the old blacktop and dispose of broken pieces.

- Grade the driveway bed down to 5 or 5½ inches below garage door. If you have had a drainage problem, resolve it now before you pour.

- Set 2″ × 4″ forms. (Nail stakes outside forms.) If you have a turning circle or curve, use redwood benders. Set spaces for brick strips to act as expansion separators.

- Add a bed of sand. I used 2 inches of sand and 3½ inches of concrete. Check your municipal building codes.

- Make arrangements with your local ready-mix concrete company to find a finisher. Have him check out your forms construction and help you determine how much concrete you'll need.

- Have ready-mix company pour concrete and assist finisher. Ask about Hunt's Process to eliminate need for periodic spraying over several days.

- When the concrete is dry remove 2″ × 4″s carefully, so you don't chip concrete.

- Mix mortar and set bricks in the divider spaces across driveway. Clean off bricks with sponge.

DRY STONE WALL

A stone wall adds a charm to a home that no other structure can match. However, it is often constructed because it provides a solution to a problem: Where else can you put all that loose stone you have lying around? Or it may be constructed because a homeowner has easy access to a large supply of stone, called rocks in some parts of the country.

The wall described here is specific to a garden enclosure adjacent to a used brick addition to the coauthor's old rock house in Galena, Illinois. It provides a back entrance, through a wooden gate, to a flagstone patio and screened-in porch behind the house. The procedure for building is the same for a straight or curved dry stone wall.

There is no shortage of limestone in a town built in a valley, on a series of limestone ledges. But the supply for this particular wall, and a perimeter wall as well, came from an unlimited supply, dumped into my own yard.

To shorten a complicated story, some years ago the city hired a local contractor to put in a water line running down the street (a steep hill) adjacent to my house on a large corner lot. There was a dip in my lawn, which sloped down the hill toward another street. I thought it might be neat to build up the slope, so I invited the contractor to dump in a few loads of fill dirt.

At that time I lived in the city, three hours away from the house, which was uninhabited during the trench digging. In addition to being just plain ignorant, there were a couple of specific things I didn't know: mainly that there was no dirt, only pieces of limestone shale. I also didn't know that the contractor would use the lot as a construction dump until a neighbor called a halt. (But then I asked for it, didn't I?)

Some years later when a front-end loader operator was out of a job, he and a friend used the bigger (200-500 pound) pieces of limestone to build a wall around the lot perimeter. The rest of it was piled in a corner mound from which we mine rock as we need walls constructed. The wall pictured is one such, built by John Becker, a local brick and stone contractor, and his partner, in one day.

Here's how to do it.

Dig a Trench

Stake out the outer perimeter of your wall with a mason's line at the ground level. Then determine the approximate thickness of your wall and mark that point with a stake. Now add another line at the approximate height you plan to build the wall. Let's say it's to be 3 feet high.

Next, dig a shallow trench about 8 to 10 inches deep and a bit wider than the anticipated thickness of your wall. (The thickness should be roughly equal to the height.) The trench will serve two purposes: to lock in the foundation course, but more important, to allow you to adjust for differences at ground level. Just measure from the bottom of your trench to the mason's line and add 8 to 10 inches to get your 3 feet of wall height from ground level. I should point out at the start that these figures are approximate because you're working with random size stones, but the top of your wall should be as level as you can reasonably make it.

Collect Your Stones

Start putting together a pile of stones near your work site. There are many kinds and shapes of stones, and if there is one constant, it is this: They're all heavy. Depending on the size of your stones, you may have to rent a loader. At the very least you'll need a wheelbarrow, and you should wear heavy work gloves.

Put aside flat stones for the top of your wall and keep some big pieces for the foundation course; however, you should distribute the sizes of stone throughout the wall. Don't put all the biggest ones on the bottom and the smallest on top. Balance them so the end result will look pleasing to the eye.

If you're building an L-shaped or U-shaped wall, keep the square pieces for the corners, especially on the bottom course. Also segregate the long pieces for use as bond stones to run the thickness of the wall, from front to back.

Start Laying Stones

Use a course of big, flat, and square stones — if you have them – for the bottom course. If one piece

is slanted on the bottom, you can prop up one end with a wedge-shaped piece and level out the face. The thickness of your wall will depend on the height and the kind of stones used. Obviously, flat limestone will provide a more solid base than rounded granite fieldstone. (In the U-shaped wall shown here, we used limestone which shales in flat strips, with some pieces big enough to provide the full thickness of the wall.) Lay your long bond stones about every 7 or 8 feet to provide additional strength. Fill in the spaces in the center with small stones. If you do any forcing of stones into spaces, use a rubber mallet. If you want to chip off pieces to make the stone fit better, use a brick set and mason's hammer and make certain you are wearing safety glasses.

When you lay your second course, make sure that the spaces between the stones are not lined up directly above the spaces below; the courses should be staggered, like a brick wall. You should also slope the second course back from the foundation course, both front and back. Do the same with each successive course so that the top course is less thick than the foundation course. This diminishing thickness slope is called the "batter" and provides a stronger wall since gravity, rather than mortar, holds the wall together.

If you can, use flat cap stones for the top course, and as much as possible, keep the top of the wall level. If you live in the snowbelt, ice and snow will force some of the pieces out of alignment but these can be easily replaced.

FLAGSTONE PATIO

The principle here is the same as laying a patio with brick, but there are some special considerations when working with flagstone. This is the procedure to follow for a 10′ × 14′ rectangular patio. You can make simple adjustments for your own space.

Purchase Flagstone

After you carefully measure and plot out the area of your project, take a trip out to a materials supply yard and look around. Then talk with the dealer and tell him what you plan to do. Check out the selections of flagstone. Depending on your area, you could have a choice of sandstone, limestone, or even slate, for example, and often a selection of colors. The dealer can tell you the advantages and disadvantages of each and how much stone you'll need. You can also order your sand and have it delivered at the same time as the flagstone.

Remove Dirt

Stake out the area on all four sides and remove the dirt or sod to make a level surface approximately 4 inches deep. (If you're removing sod, that's just about the right depth.) The surface of your excavated area should be quite level and should slope slightly away from the house.

Set 2″ × 4″ Forms and Fill with Sand

For building purposes a stud is generally considered to be 7′ 8⅝″ long, but you can buy 2″ × 4″s in 8, 10, 12, or 14-foot lengths. To avoid butting together, you'll need two 14-foot and two 10-foot lengths. Set the 14-foot length nearest the house and stake it securely. Use four 12-inch stakes and drive them into the dirt, *outside* the form; one at each end and the other two spaced evenly between the ends. Nail the stud to the stakes. Use your level to make sure the form is true. Then set the opposite form but make this about ½ inch lower than the one nearest the house. This is so the water will drain away from the house.

Next, set the two 10-foot end pieces of 2″ × 4″ and stake them securely. Use your level to make sure the completed forms are true and the inside measures 10′ × 14′ — if that's the size you have chosen.

Co-author Pete Peterson hired a local stonemason to lay a 78 × 12 foot sandstone patio behind the length of his stone house in Galena, Illinois. Since the width of the patio varied and there was a raised outcropping of a limestone ledge at one end, the flagstone was laid on a bed of sand without forms. Cut stone was used to construct a free-form edging for a step-up level to accommodate the 4 inch high outcropping.

NOTE: If you plan to leave the forms in place, use Wolmanized lumber or redwood. If you intend to plant grass and to let the sod hold the flagstones in place, you can use ordinary lumber which can be removed when the sod has grown.

Shovel in sand to fill the enclosed area, slightly more than flush with the top of the forms.

Build a Screed

If your formed-in area is 10′ × 14′ use the following figures to build a screed. Otherwise adapt to your dimensions. Take your 12-foot length of 2″ × 4″ and cut it to a length of 10′ 8″. Then mark off 4 inches at each end with a pencil. Measure the thickness of the flagstone and cut a notch at each end of the 2″ × 4″ — ¼ inch less than the thickness of the flagstone. For example, if your flagstone is 2 inches thick, cut a notch 1¾ inches. Your stone will vary at least ¼ inch in thickness and you'll need that tolerance to tap the thicker pieces into the sand so they stay flush with the surrounding pieces.

Level the Sand

Place your screed across the 10-foot end of the form, kneel in the sand, and pull the screed toward you. Unlike bricks, which you lay one course at a time, you should screed the entire area for laying flagstone. When all of the sand has been leveled, tamp down the sand with a small piece of planking. A 2-foot long piece of 2″ × 8″ lumber will work fine. This will put your sand level lower than you want, so you'll have to add more sand and repeat the screeding. The tamping and double screeding are extra work, but the effort will provide a stable surface and help ensure that the flagstone settles evenly.

Make a Dry Run

Here's another step that will seem like doubling your work, but it will reduce the amount of cutting and allow you to preview your work. Mark out an area about the same size as your patio and lay out the flagstone in a dry run. Do the perimeter first, using the straight edges for the outsides. Try to fit the pieces together so they fit like a jigsaw puzzle, leaving a gap of no more than 2 inches between each piece.

You'll still have to do some cutting so here's the easiest way to do it. Draw a line (or scratch the surface with a nail) where you would like the cut to be. Then stand the flagstone on edge, between your knees. Hold a small sledgehammer behind the cut with your left hand, and take a mason's hammer with your right hand and tap along the edge. Don't hit along the line; chip off the pieces until you reach the line. You can use that technique to rough out any sort of shape. Save any large pieces that chip off to fill in odd-shaped pieces in your jigsaw puzzle. Continue your dry run until all the test area is filled in, roughly the way you want.

Lay the Flagstone

Pick up the pieces in your test area and transfer them to your formed-in patio. Transfer one piece at a time to the corresponding part of your staked-out area. Start at one end and work your way to the other end. You'll have to walk on your nice smooth surface, but you can do touch-up re-screeding if necessary. (Another option: If you have a long foot-wide plank, place that across the forms and work from that.) When you have the larger pieces laid, fill in the smaller spaces with broken pieces of flagstone.

The flagstone surface should be level with the top of your forms. If one piece is thicker than the rest, use a rubber maul to tap it into the sand so it is level with the surrounding pieces. When all of the flagstone has been placed, fill in the cracks with sand and sweep clean.

Cement Bed Option

Instead of laying the flagstone in sand, you can use a bed of cement, which is simply mortar — 1 part cement to 3 parts sand. You will still need the forms, just as you would for a sand bed. And you'll still need about an inch of sand which will allow you to pour about 2½ inches of cement on top. Fill it to the top of the form. You can mix your cement in batches as you need it because you should only pour about 3 feet at a time. Then screed off the cement, level with the top of the form. Here you should use your 12-foot 2″ × 4″ in the upright position (the 2-inch side up), and you don't need to notch the ends.

Next, lay your flagstone in the wet cement. It's even more important to have all of your stone cut before you start. Mix your cement as you need it; one batch should cover a 3-foot section.

When all of the flagstone has been laid, the next step is to mix mortar for the joints. You can wait until the cement has dried so you can walk on the flagstone or, if you like, continue working from the plank and keep on going.

Mix the mortar slightly drier than the cement bed. It should be dry so that you don't stain the flag-stone. Use a pointing trowel and fill the joints flush with the top of the stone. Do one section at a time because you will get mortar on the stone and you

should clean it off as soon as you can with a damp sponge. Rinse the sponge repeatedly so all of the excess is removed and you don't wipe the dirt back onto the stone. Continue until finished.

If you use a cement bed you won't need the forms to hold the flagstones in place once the cement has dried, so these can be removed — carefully — when everything has set. Just remove the stakes and the 2″ × 4″ forms will come free.

SUMMARY

- Stake out area of project and remove dirt.
- Set forms and fill with sand.
- Screed sand level.
- Make a dry run with the flagstone.
- Cut pieces to fit like jigsaw puzzle.
- Lay flagstone pieces and fill in with sand.

For cement bed option:

- As above but fill form with cement instead of sand.
- Lay pieces in wet cement.
- Fill in between the pieces with mortar.

BRICK PLANTER

I built this planter for a customer recently. It's a good project to sharpen your bricklaying skills and it's not very expensive. Here are a few points to consider before you start.

1. These plans call for the planter to be built up against the side of your house. If you want to build it away from your foundation, simply add the back wall.
2. Dimensions shown here are 10 feet long, 2 feet high, and 2 feet deep. You can easily adapt these measurements to fit your own house.
3. CAUTION: Don't build it up to the wood siding of your house because moisture will cause the wood to rot.

Measure the Planter

Measure the length of your proposed planter along the side of your house at the line where the wood siding meets the concrete foundation. That line will be level, regardless of how the land slopes.

Let's say that you have a 2½-foot foundation on your house, measuring up from the soil line to the bottom of your siding. Measure down 6 inches from the bottom of the siding, at each end of your proposed planter. Draw a line at this point, 10 feet long. This will be the top of your planter.

At each end, drop a vertical plumb line. You can mark it with a stake or draw a pencil line on the foundation. It's your back mark so that you can lay three dry bricks, end to end, out from the side of the foundation. Allow a finger's width spacing between each and you will have your depth of two feet. (Actually 26½ inches.) Then drive a 3-foot stake at each end and secure a 10-foot mason's line to keep you on the straight and narrow as you lay your bricks. Your mason's line should be on level with the back line drawn on the foundation. To make it easy to keep each course straight, put a mark at 3-inch intervals on each stake, starting with the top and working to the soil line. Then you can set your mason's line at each level as you lay your courses.

If you lay a couple of dry bricks along the front line and stack eight bricks on one of them, you'll have a good idea of how high it will be. If this approximate size (10′ × 2′ × 2′) looks O.K., you'll need about 154 bricks, but you should buy a dozen more because you'll have to cut some.

Compute the number of bricks you'll need as follows:

2′ deep × 2′ high = 4 sq. ft. each end × 2 ends = 8 sq. ft.

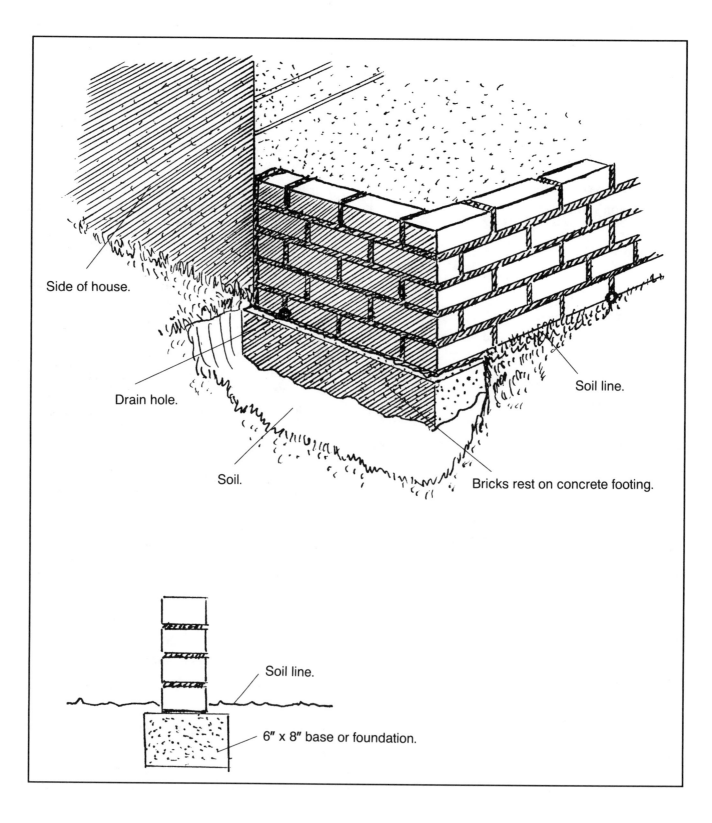

Side of house.

Drain hole.

Soil.

Soil line.

Bricks rest on concrete footing.

Soil line.

6" x 8" base or foundation.

10′ long × 2′ high = 20 sq. ft. This front wall, plus each end = 28 sq. ft. We figure that it takes 5.5 bricks for each square foot and that comes to 154 bricks.

Dig Your Trench

Stake out your lines and dig a trench for your first course. Dig it about 10 inches deep so that the top of your concrete base (which we'll get to next) will be just below the level of soil. Make the trench about 8 inches wide. If your land slopes you will have to dig deeper at one end.

This is how I set my mason's line. I drive a wood stake at each end and tie on a strong string. We use a regular mason's cord that won't break. The line is level with the top of the first course, and a line's thickness in front of the brick. Then I put a 3-inch mark for each course I have to lay. I do this on each stake and simply move up the mason's line one notch for each course.

Set a Concrete Base

Mix enough concrete to make a base on which you should lay your first course of bricks. The base should be 6 inches high and 8 inches wide. The formula for mixing concrete is 1 part cement, 3 parts sand, and 3 parts pea gravel. For this particular planter you will need about ½ ton each of gravel and sand.

You should make the mix a bit stiff so that you can start laying bricks immediately after pouring without waiting for it to dry overnight . . . if you prefer. (Your option.) If you continue after pouring your base, press the first course bricks into the hardening base about ¼ inch. If you let it harden, you'll have to lay ½ inch of mortar on the base. Then press the brick into the mortar about ⅛ inch, to make the standard ⅜-inch bed joint.

Start Laying Bricks

You'll have to mix up a batch of mortar first, of course. You might start with one bag of cement and three bags of sand. If you need more you can mix it later. The trick is to keep your mortar and bricks as close to your work area as possible.

If you are right-handed, start at the left and work to your right. Use a level to make certain that your bricks are even.

You will have to cut bricks for your second course; specifically the brick that fits up against the foundation, and for this you should have what we call a brick set. It's actually a short 5-inch wide chisel. One short tap on the brick set with a hammer will usually split the brick with a clean break. You need the half brick so that you will have staggered joints, as your courses progress.

After you lay your second course, take your tuck-pointer and run it through the head joint at every fifth or sixth brick, to remove the mortar and make a hole. This will allow drainage and prevent the soil from getting sour. (When the planter is built and you begin to fill it with top soil before planting, throw a handful of gravel in behind each of these drainage holes to keep them from getting clogged with dirt.)

When you have reached your height (and again, it should be at least 6 inches below the top of your foundation — otherwise you could have water leakage problems inside your house), make sure that the mortar joints on the top course are full and smooth. You can strengthen the walls of your planter by plastering the inside. Hold the top of the brick on the top course to compensate for the side pressure. Then, using your trowel as a plastering tool, apply a layer of mortar on the inside of the planter. You should go all the way down but make sure that the drain holes are open.

Clean Off the Bricks

Use a sponge to wipe off the excess mortar. You will have to go over and over each brick to make sure it's clean. In a short while a white haze will

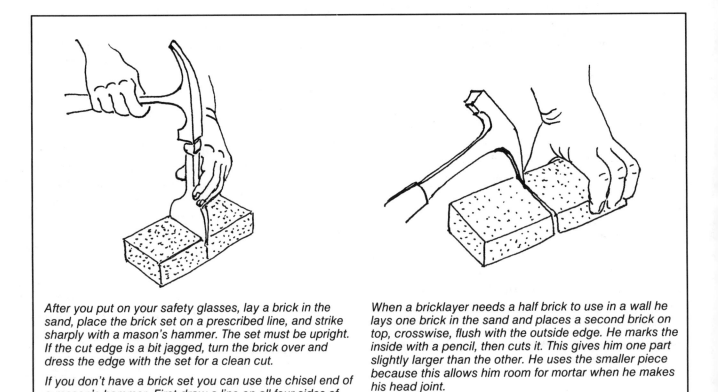

After you put on your safety glasses, lay a brick in the sand, place the brick set on a prescribed line, and strike sharply with a mason's hammer. The set must be upright. If the cut edge is a bit jagged, turn the brick over and dress the edge with the set for a clean cut.

If you don't have a brick set you can use the chisel end of a mason's hammer. First draw a line on all four sides of the brick. Then score along your line. Tap lightly around all four sides. Keep doing that until the brick splits.

When a bricklayer needs a half brick to use in a wall he lays one brick in the sand and places a second brick on top, crosswise, flush with the outside edge. He marks the inside with a pencil, then cuts it. This gives him one part slightly larger than the other. He uses the smaller piece because this allows him room for mortar when he makes his head joint.

appear which you can clean off with a dry towel. If the haze persists you can use the half of sponge rubber ball.

Allow at least twenty-four hours for the mortar to harden before filling the planter and backfilling the first course. Even after the garden is planted, you'll probably look at your brickwork first, then the flowers.

SUMMARY

- Measure space and lay out one course of dry bricks to check size.

- Dig 6-inch deep ditch for first course and set mason's line.

- Mix concrete and pour 6-inch high, 8-inch wide base.

- Mix mortar.

- Set first course on concrete base.

- Put in drain holes at second course.

- Lay bricks to predetermined height.

- Clean off excess mortar.

- Backfill and wait twenty-four hours before filling planter.

HERRINGBONE PATTERN PORCH AND WALK

TOOLS & MATERIALS NEEDED

- ☐ Bricks
- ☐ Concrete (cement, sand, pea gravel)
- ☐ Grout — silica sand and Portland cement
- ☐ Grout sealer
- ☐ 2″ × 6″ boards
- ☐ 2″ × 4″ studs
- ☐ Stakes
- ☐ Hammer and nails
- ☐ Electric powered diamond saw with water attachment (rent)
- ☐ Cement mixer (rent)
- ☐ Brick trowel
- ☐ Squeegee and handle
- ☐ Sponges and water bucket

The dimensions and conditions for your specific project will probably differ from the exact size of the job explained here. However, the steps and techniques will remain the same, so it will not be difficult to adapt your project to the one described as follows. As you can see from the photograph showing the finished job, the result is well worth the effort.

One note of caution before you start: This herringbone pattern requires cutting a lot of bricks as you'll see from looking carefully at the finished job photographs. You will need to rent special equipment to handle this.

Set Forms for Porch

First, determine the length and width of the porch. Then, excavate any soil that must be removed and set forms for your concrete. The forms should be made with 2″ × 6″ boards of sufficient length, and they should be securely staked on the outside. By all means buy and use the wood stakes that are designed for this job.

The back form will be against your house, under the door sill. The top of the form should be 3½ inches below the bottom of your entry door sill. This is so the top of the brick laid on the concrete slab will be flush with the bottom of the sill. The front form should be about ¾ inch below the back form. This is so water will run away from the house. Use your level to set your side forms to accommodate this slight pitch. (NOTE: We had an L-shaped house so we only need two side forms.)

The concrete slab for our porch was 5′ × 7′ and was 6 inches deep, which totals 17.5 cubic feet. (1 cubic yard = 27 cubic feet.)

Set Forms for the Walk

Set your mason lines to determine the exact length and width and pitch that you want. Excavate whatever soil that is necessary. This will be about 4 inches deep all along the walk. This should have a slight fall toward the street so you don't get rainwater running toward the house. You should use 2″ × 4″ studs here because you only need 3½ inches of concrete.

If you have to join together two 2″ × 4″s when setting up your form, here's an easy way to do it.

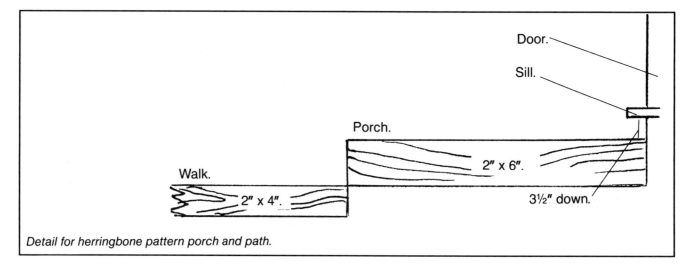

Detail for herringbone pattern porch and path.

Butt the two ends together and nail on a 1″ × 4″ splint on the *outside*.

The 2″ × 4″ studs at the beginning of the walk (the point where it ties in with the porch) should be tucked *under* the bottom of the 6″ form that marks the outside edge of the porch. This is to allow a 6-inch step up to the porch. Secure the parallel forms with stakes on the outside of the 2″ × 4″s. You will have to dig out the soil at this point to fit under the 6-inch form and probably all along the walk to get the proper grade.

Pour Concrete

Our walk was 25 feet long and 4 feet wide. This is 33.4 cubic feet which, added to our 17.5 cubic feet for the porch, equals 51 cubic feet or 1.9 (say 2) cubic yards. Your job might be more . . . or less.

You have the option to rent a mixer or order the concrete from a ready-mix plant. Check the price from your local plant and let them know the dimensions of your project. They will help you figure your needs and give you a price for the job. They will only charge you for the amount delivered, but there is usually a penalty for a short load. A standard load varies depending on where you live; in our area it's 9½ yards, in yours, probably less.

Compare this to the cost of renting a powered cement mixer and purchasing the dry cement, sand, and gravel. If you mix your own concrete, the proportions are 1 part cement, 3 parts sand, and 3 parts pea gravel. We used a short load of ready-mix, sometimes called transit mix.

Use a 5-foot length of 2″ × 4″ as a screed to level off the top of your walk. Make a "sawing" motion, pulling toward you across the top of your 2″ × 4″ form. Keep pulling the concrete toward you. This is to even out the concrete and also to rough up the surface so the bricks will adhere better.

You'll need a longer length of screed for your concrete porch area, but this must also be leveled off and roughed up slightly for better bonding.

After the screeding is done, let it set overnight.

After you remove the forms it's worth your while to clean off your 2″ × 4″ and 2″ × 6″ forms and store them for future use.

Start with the Porch

Mix a batch of mortar — 1 part cement mix and 3 parts sand. Move your materials into place and start to lay bricks.

Lay two courses of bricks around the perimeter of

the porch. The top of your second course should be flush with the top of your concrete slab porch. To make sure that this happens, first lay your bricks out dry to see how much mortar you'll have to put below the bottom of the first course. It will probably be about an inch if you allow a normal ⅜ to ½ inch for your second course.

When this is done start laying a third course — a header course – across the top of the second course. Half the brick will be resting on top of your second course, half on the concrete slab. In effect it will act as a picture frame for the herringbone pattern in the center (see photo).

To make sure you retain your pitch to handle the flow of water away from the house, place a brick at each end of the porch. The front brick should be slightly lower, about ¼ inch, than the brick at the back. You'll need your level to check this.

Set your header course bricks in mortar but leave your head joints — the space between your bricks — open, for now. You'll fill these in later.

Set Herringbone Pattern Inside Your Frame

As stated earlier, this pattern requires cutting bricks; more cutting than you can reasonably do with a masonry blade attachment for your power saw. You'll need to rent an electric-powered diamond saw with a water attachment — one where running water cools off the blade.

This equipment must be used with caution because you are using electricity with water. You obviously shouldn't stand in the water while you're operating the saw. And it's mandatory that you use the three-prong plug and an outlet that will accommodate it to make sure the equipment is properly grounded. In fact, it might be best if you hire a professional to handle this phase of the job. In any event, make certain that you are properly checked out at the equipment rental store. You might also have to wear an apron because the saw throws a spray of

water while you're working. It goes without saying, you *must* wear safety glasses.

The saw comes with a table that has rollers which guide the brick being cut. It takes two men to move the portable unit.

Here's how to make the first cut. Place a full brick on the slab. Lay another brick across it, flush with the top edge, and draw a pencil mark across the bottom brick. Take the smaller part (which is less than half a brick) and draw a diagonal line from one corner to the other. Make your first cut on that line to get a triangular piece of brick.

Next, make a mark halfway across the front end of the porch. Since our porch is 7 feet wide, your mark will be at 3½ feet. Place your triangular piece on top of that mark for the start of your herringbone pattern. To get the feel of the pattern, place the first few bricks on dry. Then mortar the bottom but leave the joints open.

The remainder of your cut brick should be placed alongside your triangle, then set a third brick going the opposite way of the cut brick. Next, place four bricks alongside each other, like parked cars. Place the next two bricks on top going in opposite directions. (NOTE: It's much easier to show you than tell you, so consult your diagram frequently.) Adjust these bricks so the exterior is flush on all four sides. The opening that remains on top is the width for all joints. Cut a piece of ½-inch plywood or any appropriate board and use this as a template for your spacing.

All of your bricks should be set in mortar but leave the joints open. Start in the front and work toward the door. And, at this point, don't walk on your work. All of this cutting and mortaring is slow going so don't expect to finish in a short work session. When you decide to quit for the day, remove the excess mortar. Then take a sponge and water and wash off the top of the bricks that you've laid. When you start up again the next day, you

Concrete slab entrance to front door.

The top of the second course (above the concrete walk) should be flush with the concrete slab porch.

Lay header course frame of bricks before setting diagonal pattern of bricks inside.

Set bricks in mortar but leave the joints open for grout.

Lay header course on the walk first, before filling in the interior.

It's a lot of work but the result is worth the effort.

can lay down a sheet of plywood to distribute your weight and work from that.

Through trial and error, you will devise your own system for the best way to cut brick since each piece and cut will vary from the next. You'll have to check your patterns constantly to make sure you're right. One test is that no straight joint should be longer than a brick and a half. If you're careful, no problems should arise.

About Grout

After all of your porch bricks have been laid, let them sit overnight before you begin to grout, or fill in, your header joints. But before you do this, it will be well worth your while to apply grout release on the bricks. This is a clear liquid used to prevent mortar from staining the face of the bricks. You can buy it at your materials yard, or many hardware stores. It's fairly expensive — anywhere from $12 to $20 a gallon. You can easily apply it with a medium nap roller. It dries fast so you can apply a second coat right after the first. (NOTE: Grout release may be called by another name in your area, so be sure to describe what you need it for.)

Next, mix your grout which, for this project, is simply a loose mortar. Mix 2 parts sand (#30 silica sand, if possible) and 1 part Portland cement. This is a much richer mix than normal because when you wash off the bricks in your next step, you'll weaken the joints. Mix the grout to the consistency of thick soup. When it's thoroughly mixed, shovel it in a bucket and pour from the bucket on top of your bricks.

You'll find it easier to apply the grout with a squeegee — the kind that you use to clean windows, with a 12- to 15-inch blade, mounted on a long handle. Move the grout around until all the joints are filled. You will need several applications because you'll find that the grout shrinks. So it's best to do a small section at a time.

Sponge Off

You'll need a 5-gallon bucket of clear water and several sponges for the final step. With a circular motion and a damp sponge, wipe off the mortar from the top of your bricks. Do it lightly and work at an angle so that you fill all the joints. Alternating sponges, concentrate on one brick at a time. It's okay to work on top of your bricks at this time if the mortar under your bricks has set overnight or longer.

Continue sponging until the porch is clean. Then you're ready to tackle the walk.

The Walk

The perimeter of the walk is handled the same as the porch. First, all forms should be removed. Then set two bricks at either end, on one side of the walk, in a header position, i.e., across the walk. Use your level to make sure the bricks are true. Now stretch a mason line on the front and back sides of the bricks. With two lines you'll be able to prevent the bricks from tipping. Then repeat the process on the other side of the walk.

Lay your bricks in mortar on either side, using your mason lines as guides. Then lay a course of bricks at the ends of the walk, this time running with the walk. You now have a brick frame around the walk (see photo).

Next, fill in the interior of the walk. Start with the same 45 degree diamond cut that you did to start off the porch. Then continue the pattern. You'll find that there are many cuts to make but the finished result is pleasing to the eye. Remember, as you are laying your pattern, to use the 2″ × 4″ tamp to level with the outer edging.

You're bound to slop some mortar on the face of your brick and you should clean it off with a damp sponge before it hardens. After the walk is completed, let it dry overnight.

The next day (or next work session) apply two coats of grout release to prevent the grout from sticking to the face of the bricks. Then mix the grout (as you did before — 2 parts #30 silica sand to 1 part cement) and pour a small section at a time. As you did with the porch, pour and clean a small section at a time.

Continue until completed and wait for a couple of days before you walk on it. What you have built will remain a thing of beauty for the life of the house.

SUMMARY

- Set dimensions for porch, removing soil if necessary.
- Set form for porch.
- Excavate soil and set forms for walk.
- Pour concrete for porch and walk.
- Remove form and lay frame of bricks around perimeter of porch.
- Use diamond saw for cutting bricks.
- Set herringbone pattern inside frame.
- Fill in joints with grout. Use grout release to protect face of bricks.
- Clean off bricks.
- Lay bricks in walk.
- Clean off bricks.

SECURITY FENCE

The beauty of this type of fence is that it keeps out unwanted visitors but doesn't shut you off from the world. It's a combination of adobe block columns with 10-foot wrought iron fencing units set between the columns and mounted on an adobe block base. In our area this is ideal for pool security for which the code calls for a 5-foot barricade around the pool, with self-closing gates. A homeowner can build the base and columns, but the wrought iron fence units are generally fitted professionally.

Measure the Projected Wall

Stake out the line where your wall is to be built so you can approximate the number of blocks you'll need. The plans described here are for a wall with 10-foot spaces between the columns for wrought iron fencing. You should check on the availability of this type of fencing in your area. You might intend to have the fencing custom-made for this specific project, in which case you can pretty much determine the width and height. However, the spacing should provide a pleasing symmetry. You should also remember to start and end the fence with a column to provide a support for the wrought iron fencing. If you can purchase ready-made fencing, you might be locked into what is available. NOTE: If you want a gate, you should check on the availability of this as well.

Purchase Blocks

I used tan adobe block, which gives a softer, more attractive appearance than concrete block. Talk over your plans with the salesperson at your materials yard and let him show you what's available. If he doesn't have what you want, perhaps he can order it.

When ordering block, the width is always mentioned first. This wall uses two sizes of adobe block — for the columns and the base. The column size is 12-4-12 — 12 inches wide, 4 inches high, and 12 inches long. This type has one 8-inch square hole, unlike the two or three holes in standard concrete block. The hole spacing is important for placing vertical reinforcing rods. You will also need a cap or flat piece for topping off each column (12-2-12).

The base, which runs between the columns and below the wrought iron fencing, uses a different size block. These are less visible and can be less expensive. They are 6-4-16 — 6 inches wide, 4 inches high, and 16 inches long. Since the base only goes two courses high, no steel reinforcing rod is needed. The first course, which is placed wet in the concrete footing, is standard adobe block with two holes. The second course is the same dimension but solid (no holes), to give the wall a finished look.

For the base you need seven blocks of each type, plus one half block of each type. No cutting will be necessary. Half blocks are available at the materials yard. (Seven blocks × 16 inches long = 112 inches, plus one half block of 8 inches = 10 feet long.)

Dig Trench

Stake out the dimensions so your wall will follow a straight line. I dug 12 to 14 inches deep. Check the municipal codes for the depth in your area. The trench should be 12 to 14 inches wide. Each 10-foot section should be level, but if the land slopes, each section can be stepped to adjust to the elevation of your property.

Put in Steel

Reinforcing steel comes in a variety of sizes and is sold commercially in 20-foot lengths, but you can get them any length you want. You'll need the ⅜-inch diameter size, and you will have to determine the quantity you'll need depending on the length of your wall — after you go over this section.

You will need two 10-foot pieces laid horizontally, for every 10-foot section of the wall. The steel shouldn't touch dirt, so put them on 2″ × 2″ concrete spacers. The spacers are made for this purpose and have a wire for securing the steel. The steel should overlap the steel from the next section for a total of two feet. If the next section is stepped up, you can easily bend the steel to make the rise and allow your overlap. You will have to cut off the end bars to fit the last section because of the overlap. They can be easily cut with a hacksaw.

At this point, you should double check the positioning of your columns. To make certain you have the exact spot, place a dry block at each 10-foot interval. There should be 10 feet between each block.

Each column will need two upright pieces of ⅜-inch steel. These must be secured to the horizontal steel, at the proper intervals. Each upright should be about 3 feet long, with a 4-inch bend at the bottom to fit under the horizontal steel in the trench. Secure it with wire, and make sure no part is touching the dirt. Since the bottom of the steel is secure but the top is not, you'll have to temporarily prop up the reinforcing rods.

Pour the Concrete Footing

No form is need for pouring the concrete because you're just filling up the trench. However, depending on the length of your fence, you will probably need more concrete than you can mix and handle by hand. You can rent a cement mixer but a load of ready-mix (also called transit-mix) concrete will be much easier, even though it will probably be a short load, for which you will pay a premium. If your trench is about 12″ × 12″ (as mine was), each running foot is a cubic foot and thus 27 feet is one cubic yard. Figure 25 feet per yard and compute how many yards of concrete you'll need. If you use ready-mix make sure you have easy access to the trench; if not, order a pump. The company will provide this for an additional fee. The driver will assist you in pouring the footing. Use a shovel to make sure it's level.

Lay the First Course

Set your first course of adobe block — the type with the two holes — in the wet concrete. Use a level and check the top both ways — with the wall and across it — then use your level vertically to make sure the blocks are plumb. After every couple of blocks use a rat-tail jointer to finish off your joints.

When you come to the end of the first 10-foot section, lift a column block over the reinforcing bar, set it on the concrete form, and level it with the preceding base wall block that you have just

Fence sections between columns are 10 feet wide.

Columns are easy to build because they use 1-hole adobe block (12" x 4" x 12"), stacked one block on top of another.

laid. Then continue with the rest of the first course base wall blocks and repeat the action at the next upright steel.

You might also consider this possibility, especially if you haven't done this type of work before. You could hire a professional bricklayer to help you with the first course; his work could also include pouring the concrete. After the first course you can't go any further until the concrete dries.

Lay the Second Course

When the concrete has been set (allow at least twenty-four hours), lay the second — and final — course. This is the solid block to finish off the wall. No reinforcing steel is needed here. You should also set the second course column block over the upright and make sure it's level with the top of the wall.

Start Columns

Since the column is only one block wide, you're stacking the one-hole adobe blocks, one on top of another, with mortar joints between them.

The mortar should be mixed with the standard 1 bag of Portland cement to 3 bags of sand and the proper amount of water. If you have any lime, add 2 shovelsful per 97-pound bag of cement for a smoother, easier-to-handle mix. (If you can buy a plastic cement, you don't need lime.)

Lay a bed of mortar on top of the last block, so that the joint will wind up about ½" to ⅝" in height. Place the block over the steel and level both ways on top, then plumb all four sides vertically. Continue on until you reach the desired height. After 3 feet, of course, you are above your reinforcing steel. (To conform with code, my columns were 5'8", including the cap, which you shouldn't set yet.)

Pour Concrete

After the columns have set (allow at least a couple of hours), you should pour concrete in the 8-inch holes to provide support to the vertical reinforcing steel rods. The mixture should be 1 part Portland cement, 3 parts sand, and 3 parts pea gravel. Fill one hole at a time so that when you are halfway down you can insert another bar of reinforcing steel. Cut it about 2 inches shorter than the top of the column. Mine was 5'6", running from the top of the footing to slightly less than the top block. Make sure the rebar does not touch the sides and is as close to the middle of the hole as possible. The steel must be completely surrounded by concrete for greatest strength.

Set the Cap

The last step is to set the cap to finish off the column. This is a 12-inch square solid piece of the same material adobe, 2 inches thick. Mortar the top block as before and set the cap on top. Level both ways and plumb so it looks level. Allow two to three days for your mortar and concrete to set and you can fit the wrought iron sections.

When it's complete, this is truly a beautiful fence. It's expensive, largely because of the wrought iron work. But you can still save a substantial part of the cost by doing the footing and columns yourself. Even if you hire a worker for a day, you'll still save at least a third over a contracted-out job.

SUMMARY

- Stake out wall.
- Determine number and kinds of blocks to purchase.
- Dig trench and put in reinforcing steel.
- Pour concrete footing.
- Lay base blocks.
- Lay column blocks.
- Pour concrete in holes with vertical steel rods.
- Set caps.

PUTTING A NEW FACE
ON AN OLD FIREPLACE

TOOLS & MATERIALS NEEDED

- ☐ 2″ × 4″ studs (4)
- ☐ Mortar — cement, sand, water
- ☐ Mixing container
- ☐ Hoe or shovel
- ☐ Trowel
- ☐ Mason's level
- ☐ Tuckpointer
- ☐ Brick set
- ☐ Hammer
- ☐ Mason's line
- ☐ 3″ angle iron
- ☐ Metal lath
- ☐ Concrete nails
- ☐ Safety glasses

If a nice cozy fireplace goes a long way toward helping you sell your home, a messy, ugly fireplace is sometimes worse than having none at all. Quite often there's nothing wrong with the way the fireplace burns, but the materials used to make it are out of sync with your decorating schemes.

Case in point: the original green (ugh), slump stone fireplace shown on page 114. The legs, or jambs, were skinny — these are the vertical sides on either side of the opening. There was also a black slate hearth that stuck up about one inch above the floor. The perfect height for stumbling over. The fireplace itself worked fine, however, and as you can see by the stains, they used it often during the southern California winters. The residence — a typical tract house — belonged to a friend who asked me to reface the family room fireplace with used brick.

Cover the Floor

To protect the area around the fireplace, cover the floor. Put down a tarp so you don't grind in dried mortar or cause the bricks to scratch the floor.

(On my own job, I also removed the slate hearth with a hammer and chisel to get it flush with floor level. Actually there was a concrete hearth below this so I just left it so I could build it up later.)

Lay Out the Width of the Fireplace

With a line of dry brick, lay out the width of the fireplace. Allow a finger's width between each for the mortar joint. When you have the proper width, set your three 2″ × 4″ frames — one on each side and one horizontally.

Make sure the upright studs are plumb (perfectly vertical), then nail them out about an inch from the wall so that the outside ends measure out about 5 inches. This will allow about an inch for mortar on the wall behind the bricks which normally are set at 4 inches deep. You will have to put wedges behind the studs to make them steady. (I used a board in back of the horizontal piece and set it at 5 inches.)

Starting at the floor, make a series of pencil marks on one of the vertical studs, 2⅞ inches apart, up to your horizontal 2″ × 4″ crosspiece. Next, do the same with the stud on the opposite side of the fireplace. Then drive a small nail in each mark. Now you can run a mason line between your pairs of nails as you lay your courses, and you know your bricks will be absolutely level. Your end bricks will also be plumb because they'll be laid snug against your studs on either side.

Start Laying Bricks

If you use full bricks for the first course, you will have to use some half bricks for the second course. Use your brick set to cut the bricks in half and put the cut end toward the wall. By using a two-brick wide jamb — the legs on either side of the fireplace opening — you only have to cut bricks every second course. Build up each side until you reach the top of the opening.

IMPORTANT: Your top course must be even with, or a little below, the top of the opening.

Set Your Angle Iron

The angle iron is a standard 3″ × 3″ piece of metal which should be cut long enough to allow an overlap of 3 inches on each side of your fireplace opening.

IMPORTANT: The angle iron must be level, so use your mason's level to make certain that it is. If it is not, build up a small amount of mortar on one side or the other to make it level. (If you have been using your nail marker mason lines you should be very close.) In addition, the angle iron should be set back ½ inch from the face so it doesn't show when you are finished. However, when you do this, two situations will occur and these require special treatment.

First, your bricks, which measure 3¾ inches, will protrude from the front of the 3 inch deep angle iron, especially when you include the mortar behind the bricks. So you must cut the bricks the long way. The technique for doing this is as follows. Measure the part needed for cutting, then mark your line with a pencil. The most efficient way for a homeowner to make the cut is to buy a carbide blade for your circular power saw. It's designed for cutting masonry and it costs under $3. You should

do this cutting job outdoors and by all means wear a mask because it is a dusty job. It's also mandatory that you wear safety goggles. The carbide blade will give you a smooth, accurate slice of brick, which is exactly what you need.

Another alternative is to use a brick set to make the cut, or as most masons do, use the sharp cutting side of a mason's hammer. Set the brick on end and chip first one end, then the other. Next, lay the brick on its side and chip away the middle part. You will get a slightly jagged cut but this side will be placed against the mortar. You will probably have to cut bricks for two courses over the opening to clear the angle iron. Then you can go back to full width.

Second, there will be a gap across the opening, between the back of the angle iron and the original fireplace face. To bridge this gap and provide a support for the next course of bricks, put in a strip of metal lath. Make an "L" shape of the metal lath. It's best to nail the lath to the original masonry and you do this with concrete nails. CAUTION: Make sure you are wearing safety glasses because the nails are very hard, and if you hit them at an angle they fly like bullets.

Then fill in the space with solid mortar.

Continue Your Courses

As you lay your brick across the face of the existing fireplace, make certain that you tie the new work to the old. A good way to do this is to bend 4-inch wide strips of metal lath and nail them to the existing masonry. Three or four strips will do the job. (We do this as an earthquake precaution, but it's sound practice for any part of the country.)

After you reach your designated height, you'll need one additional course for the mantel.

Lay Your Mantel

You'll want this course to project 1½ inches out from the face to make it a proper mantel. To do this you lay your bricks ends out from the wall. It will help to keep the projected bricks level and provide additional support if you affix a piece of 2″ × 4″ stud to your vertical frames. Nail it across the front of the fireplace, ½ inch above your last course so you can allow for the mortar joint. (This, together with the rest of the frame, will be removed when you're done.)

You will also have to cut about 1½ inches off each of the bricks in the mantel. The full 8-inch length would project too far out to hold the brick securely. The bricks could also break off if you happened to hit one at an angle. A 6½-inch deep mantel will provide plenty of room to support the large photo — with appropriate frame — of the person who laid the fireplace.

Clean Up Your Joints

You might like to do some of this as you go along. On a relatively small job, I prefer to wait until I'm finished laying bricks. To do it properly, you need two tools. The first is a scorpion, with an adjustable nailhead which can be set to whatever depth you want. This is used to rake out the excess mortar. (On this particular job, mine was set at ¼ inch.) A tuckpointer is used next to give the joint a tooled, professional look.

Clean Off the Bricks

First, remove the forms so you can get in to clean the ends of your fireplace. You're not finished laying bricks yet, but it will be easier to clean up at this time because you can get closer to your work now than after the hearth has been laid.

Scrape off excess mortar with your trowel and/or a stiff brush and then follow up with a damp sponge. A haze will often appear on the surface of the bricks, but this can be cleaned off with a dry towel. If the haze won't come off, use the half of a sponge rubber ball, mentioned earlier.

Lay the Hearth

Your present hearth will probably be larger than the original. It should be raised from the floor so you won't fall over it, and it should be the full width of the fireplace.

Lay your new hearth over the existing hearth. To make certain that the placement of your bricks will come out right, lay out what we call a "header" course. This goes all the way around. And to make absolutely sure everything will match, lay out your header course dry, but allow the finger's width space to compensate for your mortar. You don't need a frame but set your mason lines to make sure everything is level.

First, lay out your hearth with a header course in front and on both sides. When your header course has been laid, fill in the center part with a running bond. Your first course across the opening will thus make your hearth three inches higher than your firebox. This is obviously good protection against a log rolling out during the night.

After the mortar is dry, sweep up, put your tools away, and admire your handiwork. You should allow a couple of days for the mortar to cure before lighting a fire.

SUMMARY

- Cover floor with tarp.
- Lay out width of fireplace with dry bricks.
- Set 2″ × 4″ stud frames and set nails for mason line.
- Start laying bricks to top of opening.
- Set angle iron.
- Continue with courses.
- Cut bricks for mantel course.
- Set support stud for mantel.
- Clean off bricks.
- Lay hearth.
- Clean up.

1. Lay out width of new facing with a row of dry bricks.

2. Set vertical studs. Lay 2-brick wide jambs on either side of fireplace.

3. Set angle iron, allowing 3-inch overlap on each side of opening.

4. Use strip of metal lath to bridge gap behind angle iron.

5. Bend metal lath strip into "L" shape.

6. Use a scorpion to rake out the joints.

7. Use a tuckpointer to finish the joints.

8. Lay the hearth one course high.

9. Use a header course in front.

10. Completed used brick facing.

INTERIOR ARCH

TOOLS & MATERIALS NEEDED

- ☐ 2 sheets drywall (4′ × 8′)
- ☐ Wire, for scribing arc
- ☐ Pencil
- ☐ Nails
- ☐ Mortar
- ☐ Bricks — about 60
- ☐ Jigsaw or keyhole saw
- ☐ Sawhorses
- ☐ Lengths of 2″ × 6″ lumber (two 5-foot pieces)
- ☐ Lengths of 2″ × 4″ studs (two 8-foot pieces)
- ☐ Hammer
- ☐ Brick trowel
- ☐ Tuckpointer
- ☐ Scorpion — for raking out mortar from joints
- ☐ Sponge and water

A neighbor recently put on a room addition and after I had built a fireplace for him, we discussed what to do about the doorway to the new room. He said, "I don't want to install a door because it will never be used. I'll never close it, so as far as I'm concerned it's just an open entrance to the new addition." I suggested that we make an archway to match the brick fireplace. (I should mention that the studs were exposed and we had easy access to the existing entrance.) Here's how we did it.

Scribe Arch

Buy two sheets of 4′ × 8′ drywall from your lumber yard or materials store. They're inexpensive but, because of the awkward size, you might have to have them delivered unless you own a pickup truck or station wagon.

The arch will be constructed of single bricks, with mortar joints, one on top of the other (see photo). So the first move is to measure the doorway. The one pictured here is 48″ wide × 7′ high. Deduct 9 inches from that width to make it 39 inches wide. Nine inches is the width of two bricks plus mortar; one brick's width for either side of the uprights. (If your doorway is more or less than 48 inches, you should still deduct the 9 inches from your actual width to get the working width for your arch template.)

Lay the two sheets of drywall on the floor vertically, one on top of the other. At the top of the 4-foot width, measure 39 inches out from one side, and mark a point. Do the same at the bottom and draw a line, top to bottom. Cut along this line with an X-Acto knife and discard the small piece. Make the same cut on the bottom board. Measure the height of your existing opening. (Mine was 84 inches.) Deduct 6 inches to make it 78 inches. Mark both sides of the top sheet, draw a line, and cut off the bottom. Cut both sheets, and discard the excess.

You now have two pieces of drywall, each 39 inches wide by 78 inches long. Again, place them one on top of the other. Measure across the top to find the exact center (14½ inches from either side). Mark that point and drop a ruler exactly 19½ inches from the top. Drive in a nail at this point and wrap a piece of wire around the nail. Then measure off

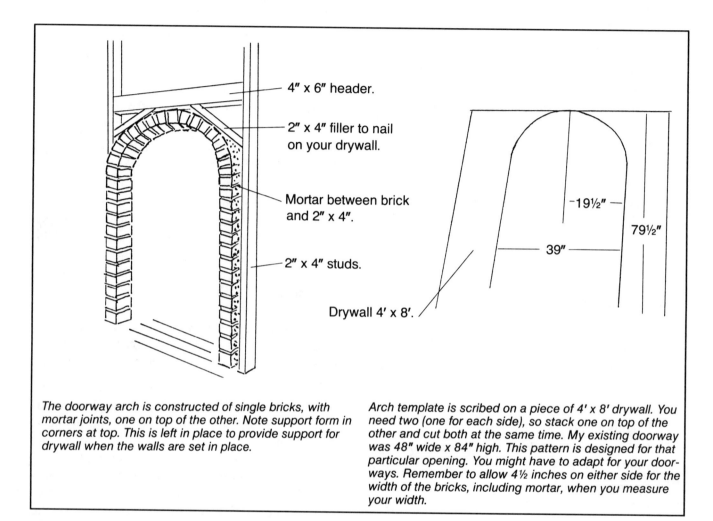

4″ x 6″ header.

2″ x 4″ filler to nail on your drywall.

Mortar between brick and 2″ x 4″.

2″ x 4″ studs.

Drywall 4′ x 8′.

−19½″−

79½″

39″

The doorway arch is constructed of single bricks, with mortar joints, one on top of the other. Note support form in corners at top. This is left in place to provide support for drywall when the walls are set in place.

Arch template is scribed on a piece of 4′ x 8′ drywall. You need two (one for each side), so stack one on top of the other and cut both at the same time. My existing doorway was 48″ wide x 84″ high. This pattern is designed for that particular opening. You might have to adapt for your door-ways. Remember to allow 4½ inches on either side for the width of the bricks, including mortar, when you measure your width.

slightly more than 20 inches, so that you can wrap the other end around a pencil and have exactly 19½ inches of wire between the nail and the pencil. That's the radius of your arc. It's best to use wire because string will stretch when you pull it taut.

Now scribe your penciled arc on the drywall (see illustration). You only need to mark one sheet because you can saw both pieces at once. Place them both on top of a pair of sawhorses and nail the two pieces of drywall inside the arc to prevent movement when you saw.

You can use a jigsaw or a keyhole saw to cut along the outline of your arc and the parallel lines to the bottom of the drywall. Then remove the nails but don't turn the pieces of arc over. You need them back to back in that same position.

Set Forms

Next take two 58½ inch pieces of 2″ × 6″ planks and place them on edge between the two pieces of template, flush with the bottom of your drywall. They should run along the edge of the drywall, up to the bottom of the arc. By using the bottom of the arc as the top position, your boards will not reach the bottom of the drywall.

With the boards between the sheets of drywall, you

now have a sandwich effect. (If this seems confusing, visualize a playing card on the table. Then put a length of pencil on either side of the playing card and place another playing card on top.) Nail one side, then the other, then turn the whole thing over and repeat the nailing process. It is important to keep the sides and the top exactly parallel.

Your form should now be 39 inches wide and 78 inches high and ready to be fitted inside the existing opening. Your bricks will then be placed between the template and the existing door jamb. But first nail two 6-foot 2″ × 4″ studs over adjacent studs on the work side of your door opening. Do this on both left and right studs.

Lay Bricks

Place your form in the center of the opening, with 4½ inches clean on each side. Set a piece of ½ inch plywood at the bottom under the form to raise it above the floor. (This will make removing it easy.) Next, nail two 8-foot lengths of 2″ × 4″ studs horizontally across the vertical studs. Nail these on both sides of the template.

To finish off your form, nail an 18-inch piece of 2″ × 4″ in each of the corners of the existing opening above the arc.

With your form in place, you're now ready to lay bricks, but you'll have a difficult time trying to work both sides of a blocked door, so cut a hole in the bottom of the form to allow access to either side (see photo). Brace the bottom of the arch with 2″ × 6″ boards.

You need enough mortar to lay about sixty bricks — about ⅓ bag of cement and one bag of sand. Now you can begin to build your arch. You will lay the bricks in a slot 4½ inches wide between the existing stud and your drywall template. Place each brick snugly against the template and put mortar at the back between the brick and the stud — enough mortar to fill the ½″-¾″ space. After you lay each brick use a level to make sure it's level.

It is important to keep the bricks level because it is a characteristic of an arch that the bricks at the top will remain in place only if the sides don't shift. It's also important to pack in a sufficient amount of mortar to keep the bricks solidly in place.

The process will be helped by working both sides. Lay five bricks on one side, then five on the other so you arrive at the arch evenly from both sides. When you approach the arch, lay the bricks right on top of the template, two on one side, then two on the other. Follow the radius of the arc. As the arc curves, so will your bricks turn, making each joint wider at the top than at the bottom. Then, when you reach the space for the last five or six bricks, place these in dry and allow ⅜ inch for a mortar joint, then mark the template with a pencil to make certain you have the right amount of space because you need full bricks. No cutting is allowed. By adjusting the joint widths you can make the arc.

When your last five or six bricks have been placed dry, make sure your mortar joints for each brick match your pencil marks, and you'll have no surprises when you lay your final brick. This last brick should be dry. Pack the joints on either side of the last brick with your tuckpointer (and your fingers if necessary) to make sure these joints are full and tight.

Remove the Template

Next, let the mortar set for about an hour and then remove the template. While you are waiting you can start cleaning up the joints on either side of your arch. At this point you have a big mess, but it's easily cleaned. First, rake out the excess ⅛ inch of mortar at your joints with a scorpion. Then run your tuckpointer across the joints to smooth them off.

Before you take out your template, remove the 1-inch wedges at the bottom and the four nails from the crosspiece, and the template will drop one inch. Then you can gently work it free. When this is

When everything is in place and forms are secure, you can cut off the center part of the drywall to allow you to work on both sides of the arch. You'll have to remove excess mortar and strike joints on the other side.

Bricks are laid up the sides and on top of the template. Work both sides evenly. Use your level often to make sure each brick is level.

done, finish fixing up your joints. Then clean off the bricks with a sponge and water. Go over and over to remove all excess mortar. After you clean up the tools and materials, you will have a work of art that will stay with the house forever.

SUMMARY

- Buy 2 sheets of drywall.
- Scribe arch and mark template.
- Cut out and nail on 2″ × 6″ wood braces in between both sheets.
- Set in place and support with 2″ × 4″ studs.
- Cut hole in bottom part to allow access to both sides of opening.
- Lay bricks, working up from either side; make sure bricks are level.
- Put up last five or six bricks dry on top of arch, to make sure you have enough room. Try to make mortar joints even.
- Set top brick in dry and pack mortar on either side.
- Let set for an hour and clean up joints with tuckpointer.
- Remove template and clean up bricks with a sponge and water.

BRICK STEPS WITH LANDINGS

TOOLS & MATERIALS NEEDED

- ☐ Shovel
- ☐ Wheelbarrow
- ☐ Mason's line
- ☐ Mason's level
- ☐ Jointer or tuckpointer
- ☐ Brick trowel
- ☐ Water bucket
- ☐ Sponge
- ☐ Garden hose
- ☐ Bricks
- ☐ Mortar (You might want to check into renting a power mixer)
- ☐ Concrete
- ☐ Railing (separate job)

The instructions and photographs that follow are specific to a custom job that I recently did at a residence near Pasadena, California. However, the procedure is the same for any set of steps built in a moderately steep incline.

Problem: This particular house was built below the street level. The attached garage has a steep driveway that made walking treacherous in wet weather. In addition, the homeowner had to use a cane for walking.

Solution: A set of brick steps with landings to ease the strain of a vertical climb. The finished job is also more pleasing to the eye than an unbroken set of steps. The length of the landings can be adapted

to fit any landscape and each is slightly pitched to allow water runoff.

Determine the Width of Your Steps

Set out your dry bricks to visualize the effect. We made ours 4½ bricks wide, which measures about 37 inches wide. (Four bricks running across the path and one with the path. See photo.) You can make your walk wider if you wish, but the width-to-length proportion should be pleasing to the eye.

NOTE: Normally we would make the path at least 42 inches wide to allow two people to pass each other, walking in opposite directions. In this instance the homeowner had a walking disability and the narrower width allowed an easy reach for the railing on either side.

Stake out the Path

Measure about 4 inches on either side of your dry bricks and drive a sturdy stake at these points on either side. Your working width should be slightly more than the actual brick width so the dirt doesn't get in your way. Then tie a mason's line (a strong cord) to a set of stakes at the opposite ends of your path. Make sure your lines are parallel because that's the course you'll follow.

Excavate the Soil

Start at the bottom and work up toward the top, digging out a rough terrace for each of the step landings. (If you are cutting out sod, you might like to keep it to patch other lawn areas. You should also keep the topsoil for garden use.)

At your first step excavation, lay down two

courses of dry brick to determine how deep your landing should be. We purposely set an easy 6-inch rise. (Under the California code the rise can be no higher than 7½ inches.) The steepness of your slope will determine the number of steps you will need.

Each step — or landing — according to these plans, has a rise of 6 inches. If you get freezing weather where you live, you should dig 1 foot deep for each step because you will need a bed of 3 inches of sand before you pour concrete. We used eleven steps or landings; the length of each landing varied to accommodate the slope. Our overall length was 25 feet.

Mix Concrete

When your terraces are dug, mix concrete and pour a 6-inch deep bed on each landing. It is not necessary to set forms since everything will be underground.

Your concrete proportions should be 1 part Portland cement, 3 parts sand, 3 parts pea gravel. Start at the bottom and work up. By the time you reach the top, the bottom step will be hard enough to lay brick. You should make your concrete a bit stiff for this phase because you are not using forms to contain it and you don't want the concrete to flow. As a general rule the drier the concrete, the stronger it will be. Concrete poured too wet will tend to break down faster.

Mix Mortar and Start Laying Bricks

Use 1 part mortar cement and 3 parts sand for your mortar mix.

Start at the base. On our job this was an existing sidewalk (see photo). The bottom of the first course is level with the top of the existing sidewalk — 4½ bricks wide.

It's best to make a dry run to be sure everything fits. Place a course of bricks around the perimeter of the bottom landing. Reset your mason's lines the exact width of your dry run bricks.

Starting at the left (if you're right-handed), place your first brick flush with your mason's line and spot the four bricks end to end across the path. Allow a finger's width spacing for your mortar joint. The fifth brick, at the right side of the step, will be set at a right angle so that it is running *with* the path. (It will look like it's a half brick as you approach the step.) The courses on each side of the path will also be laid end to end in running bond — four bricks running and one brick turned.

When everything lines up, set up a mortar stand and start laying your bricks. Work from the left mason's line and measure 37½ inches (or the width of *your* walk) out to the right. If you hold to that measurement throughout, everything will line up as you progress up the steps. Or, if you prefer, set up a line on the right and just stay between the white lines. Finish the front, then either side, making a "U", leaving the center core and back open.

You will only need one course of bricks around the border of the first step because your layer of finish brick will provide your 6-inch rise. However, all of the other steps must be two courses high (see photo).

After you have the header course on the bottom step laid, start working your way up. There is plenty of room on top of your concrete base, inside the border, to work without disturbing your newly laid courses. Each step should be 6 inches above the next.

After all borders have been laid and you reach the top, the proper procedure is to work your way down so that you don't have to walk on your work.

Fill in the Core

At this point each step will have a U-shaped border of bricks and an open concrete center. The next step is to fill in the open core flush with the top of the newly laid bricks; that's a depth of 6 inches. To make the job easier and to reduce costs, you can pour in 3 inches of sand and a layer of 3 inches of concrete on top of the sand for the rest of the steps. A wood screed will help you level the concrete, but you should take care that you don't slop over and stain the face of the bricks. If you do, clean them with a sponge and water.

Pour just 3 inches of concrete on the bottom landing and allow it to dry overnight.

Lay Your Header Course of Finish Brick

Start at the top and work down. First, mix a batch of mortar. Don't mix any more than you can use in 45 minutes to an hour; let's say a bag of Portland cement and 3 bags of sand. Mortar dries out if it stands around too long. Since you are working from the top down, it will make sense to mix your mortar at the top and wheelbarrow it down to avoid pushing a loaded wheelbarrow up the slope.

You now have a flat surface to lay your finish course. Follow the same procedure as you did earlier. That is, lay the front first, then each side. Except this time you should project the front brick ½ inch over the edge.

It will be easier if you reset your mason's lines so that you get the proper fall and pitch. One line should be slightly — say ½ inch — lower, so the rain runs off the side of your step, as well as down the slope.

Do the front and sides and keep the center open, as before. And again, leave the center core open as you work your way down the steps. When the front and sides of each step have been laid, start back at the top and fill in the center of each landing. Before you start filling in though, there is a trick to make the job look better and the work easier.

Fill in the Center

Set your first course dry inside your border, to make sure everything fits. You will note that you'll have to cut a brick every other course.

When everything fits properly, lay in a bed of mortar on top of the core and set your bricks in a running bond, but *leave the joints open*. Allow a finger's space between each and tap gently so that the top of each brick is flush with the bricks you have laid on the border. You can make certain they are flush with a length of 2″ × 4″ that fits across the step.

Fill in the center of each step using this procedure, starting at the top and working toward the bottom of the steps.

Slush in the Joints

Once again, return to the top and, using a fine spray, hose down each step. Wet the bricks thoroughly. Then mix up a final batch of mortar, but this time make it very loose so you can slush it in the joints. You can use a trowel for this and, yes, it will be a big mess. Scrape off as much of the mortar as you can from the tops of the bricks by holding the trowel at a 45 degree angle. But don't remove it from the joints.

At this point, the landing looks filthy, but go on down to the next step and repeat the process. Do about half of the steps, then go back and start your cleanup act. First, take a concave jointer or a tuck-pointer and tool joints into your first landing. Just use a slight pressure between each brick. Then go on to the next panel and continue until you have tooled joints into each step that you have slushed with your loose mortar.

The next move is to get a bucket of clean water and a sponge and wash off each brick. You may have to go over each brick several times, but you want them to look spotless — and they will.

Finally, finish the rest of the landings: Slush the loose mortar, remove the excess, make your joints, and sponge off the bricks.

Put in a Handrail

This is an optional part of this project. Allow your mortar to dry overnight and backfill the soil on the sides of your walk. In many states, building codes require a railing for this type of stair. To complete our job, I called in a contractor who specialized in wrought iron railings and asked him to do the job — as I mentioned, one on either side. I suggest you also talk to a specialist. In any event, the steps must be completed before the railing can be set.

SUMMARY

- Determine width of path and stake out mason's lines.
- Excavate rough outline of steps.
- Pour bed of concrete (layer of sand first if you live in the snowbelt).
- Lay header course border — leave center core open.
- Fill in center core — flush with border.
- Lay header course border of finish brick — leave center core open.
- Lay bricks in center — leave joints open.
- Slush joints with loose mortar.
- Clean bricks with sponge and water.
- Set railing (optional).

The bottom of the first course is level with the existing sidewalk.

All steps are two courses high.

After the border has been laid on each landing, fill in the core with sand and concrete.

Use a running bond to fill in the core. Set bricks in mortar but leave joints open. Bricks are ready to spray with water and slush in joints with a loose mortar.

Clean off the bricks with a sponge and clean water.

Finished walk with wrought iron handrail.

WATERPROOFING A BASEMENT

It's Not an Easy Job

Most older homes, and virtually all homes in the snowbelt, have a basement. A full basement provides all kinds of additional room for a family besides a place to put the furnace, hot water tank, and laundry area. A good many homeowners have installed a den or family room — or would like to — if they could only keep their basement dry.

There is a solution, of course, and that is to water-proof the *outside* wall. And, unless the water table in your backyard is up to your kitchen floor, you probably can prevent your basement from leaking. However, there is one catch. If you do it yourself, you'll still need help, but you will save a bundle. In any event, this is the procedure.

But first, before you invest considerable effort and money in fixing the exterior walls, try it the easy way — with waterproof paint inside your basement. If it works, you're way ahead. If not, you haven't lost much.

Painting contractor Jack Luts (coauthor of *The Complete Guide to Painting Your Home,* Betterway Publications, Inc., 1989) offers the following advice.

"Over the years we have successfully waterproofed basements with a product called Dry-Lok. This comes in premixed one gallon cans or 20-pound sacks of powder which is mixed with water. It's easy enough to use.

"If your basement wall has been painted, remove any loose, peeling paint first. Then dampen the wall and apply the Dry-Lok with a brush. Work it well into all the cracks and crevices. When it dries it expands and blocks out moisture. If your wall leaks a moderate amount, or only occasionally, particularly after a heavy rain, this will probably solve your moisture problems.

"Dutch Boy also puts out an oil-based waterproof paint product which is recommended for interior, unpainted concrete block basement walls or above ground exterior block or stucco surfaces. This can be applied with a brush or roller.

"You can use either of these products on a single

wall, the entire basement, or even a section of wall to test it before going further."

If you can solve your problem without the expense of digging outside your foundation, by all means experiment. But if you have continuing leakage problems, the hard way is the best, and really, the only way. Here's how to do it.

Check Your Lines

Before your backhoe operator removes any dirt, make certain that you take him into the basement to show him where your sewer, gas, and water lines run. Mark each of those lines outside the house with a stake so he won't cut into them. If you have underground electricity, mark that as well.

If you have a full basement, the first step will be to dig a trench around the side of the house where you have a leakage problem. It should be at least 2½ feet wide because you have to work in the trench, and it should be wide enough to move around in. It should extend 4 to 6 inches below the concrete footing in depth (see illustration). CAUTION: Do not go deeper. Your backhoe operator should not go below the concrete footing that the foundation is resting on because if he does, he will be removing the soil that supports the house. Usually the concrete footing is 12 to 18 inches deep. (NOTE: This part of the soil removal might best be done by hand.)

Your trench will thus be 5 or possibly 6 feet below the starting surface (depending on the height of your basement ceiling and whether you have windows in the basement). It might be even deeper if the soil removed from the trench is piled up too close to the edge. (Try to avoid this.) If your soil is sand or gravel there could be the danger of a cave-in. Clay is much safer to work in but even so, it might be a good idea to shore up the outside wall with sheets of 1-inch exterior plywood. Another way to prevent any possibility of a cave-in is to have the backhoe operator angle the trench wall

away from the house, instead of making a vertical cut.

The operator should stockpile the dirt around the top of your trench — back from the edge. You'll need it later for backfill. However, all large stones should be removed. If you can use them in your garden for decoration, great. If not, they should be removed so you don't accidentally dump them back in the trench.

NOTE: Depending on your drainage and the severity of your moisture problem you might have to excavate and treat two or even all four sides of your basement.

Brush, Mortar, and Tar

After the dirt has been removed, use your wire brush and go over the entire exposed cinderblock foundation wall and concrete footing. Wait until the dirt is dry because all of the dirt must be cleaned off. It's a slow, nasty job, but it's important that the cinderblock foundation be as clean as you can get it. After all the dirt has been wire brushed off, dust the wall. (At this stage of the job, it helps to be popular. What are friends for if you can't get them to lend a hand now and again?)

The reason the wall must be clean is simply that the foundation coating tar will adhere better to a clean wall. But first you should inspect the foundation wall to see what kind of a job the masons who built the wall did for you . . . or for the original owner. You will probably find some mortar projections at the joints. These should be removed with a hammer and chisel. (Make sure you are wearing your safety glasses.)

One reason that water is seeping into the basement in the first place is that the mortar joints leak. The water finds its way along a joint and seeps through the interior of your cinderblock basement wall. In severe conditions, the hollow cinderblock cores could fill up and water would run down your basement wall.

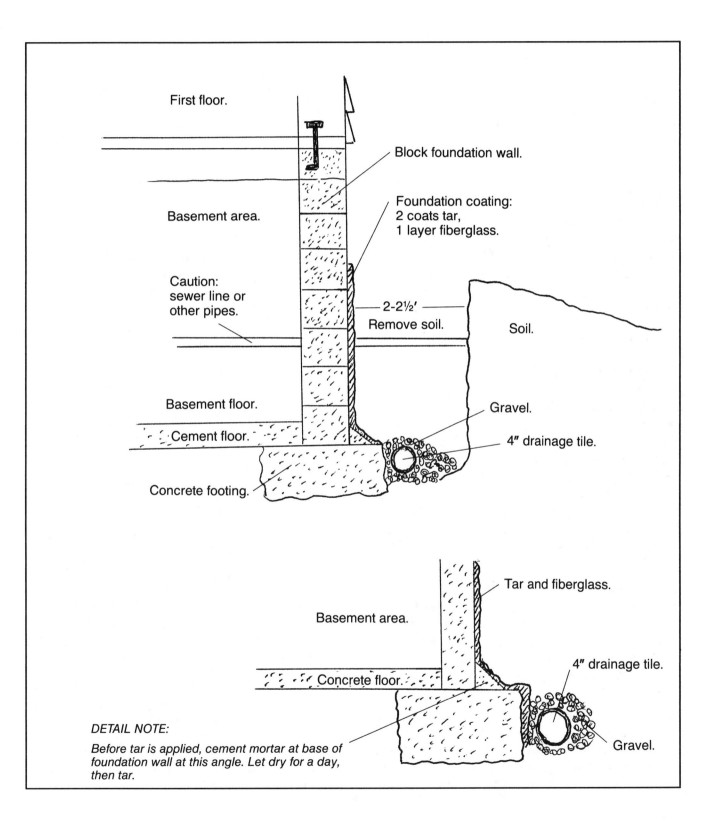

First floor.

Block foundation wall.

Foundation coating:
2 coats tar,
1 layer fiberglass.

Basement area.

Caution:
sewer line or
other pipes.

2-2½'
Remove soil.

Soil.

Basement floor.

Gravel.

Cement floor.

4" drainage tile.

Concrete footing.

Tar and fiberglass.

Basement area.

4" drainage tile.

Concrete floor.

Gravel.

DETAIL NOTE:

Before tar is applied, cement mortar at base of foundation wall at this angle. Let dry for a day, then tar.

Your first step in correcting this condition is to repair the cracked joints. You might also find small holes in the mortar joints. We call them bee holes. These small holes should also be filled with mortar. For this kind of job we use a mixture of 2 parts sand to 1 part cement to make a stiff, putty-like mortar. Then use your trowel to make the surface as smooth as you can.

Make enough mortar so that you can apply a layer at the point where the foundation wall sits on the concrete footing (see illustration). Use enough so that you can angle the mortar. Do this all around the foundation. Allow a day for the mortar to dry.

Yup, It's a Mess

The next step is to apply foundation covering. You can get this at your local building materials store. It is really a tar or asphalt that comes in 5-gallon cans and can be applied as is with a wide, inexpensive paintbrush or a three-knot brush, or even a broom. (It's a little too thick to roll on.) You'll need a lot of it: as much as 30 gallons — six 5-gallon cans — for a typical two-bedroom house.

You should start from the top, a couple of inches above the original dirt line, and really soak the foundation with tar. Fill all the holes and cover the top and exposed side of the footing. Don't use it sparingly. Go over the wall three or four times to make sure that everything is covered.

It's a messy job because you're down at the bottom, working in a confined space, sometimes above your head, sloshing on tar that spatters on your clothes. It's a good idea to wear a hat and gloves, and you might also have to throw away your shoes, shirt, and pants (or overalls) when the job is completed.

It's best to tar no more than a 6- or 7-foot section at a time and then — while the tar is still sticky — put up a 6-foot section of fiberglass or membrane tape. You can also get this at your local building supply store. (NOTE: In different parts of the country this material might be called by different names, so explain to the dealer exactly what you are doing and enlist his help.) It is similar to the 6-inch wide membrane tape that roofers use for patching roofs, except that this comes in a 3-foot wide roll and it's usually green or yellow. It's a fiber mesh that looks something like window screen and, as you'll see, it isn't waterproof in itself. Its function is to provide body to support the foundation tar, which is what actually makes your foundation watertight.

You can hang the fiberglass mesh pretty much like wallpaper, except you should overlap the edges. Press your 3-foot wide strip into the sticky tar, starting at the top of the tarred foundation, down to the footing, and then let a small projection hang over the edge. (That angled mortar layer that you applied at the bottom of the foundation allows your fiberglass strip to fit better than if you had to make a right angle tuck.)

Next, put up a second strip, overlapping the first by about 6 inches. Then go on to applying tar on the next 6-foot section of foundation.

Think of the Money You're Saving

Follow this procedure with all excavated sides of the foundation: tar thoroughly, then apply the fiberglass strips. When you have finished, apply a second coating of foundation coating over your fiberglass strips. Again, apply liberally.

It should be noted that this procedure of tarring, applying fiberglass mesh, and tarring again does take time. But it is a task that a homeowner can handle and if he does, it will substantially reduce the labor-intensive part of waterproofing the basement. What I'm saying is yes, it is slow going and it is messy, but your time spent is your money saved.

You have dug your trench 4 to 6 inches below the concrete footing. At this point, your fiberglass mesh is sticking out a couple of inches beyond the top of your footing. Underneath this fiberglass, and flush up against the exposed footing wall, start laying land or drain tile. This is actually plastic pipe, usually black, flexible hose, that runs 3 and 4 inches in diameter, and comes in sections which you can easily cut to length. Ask for the perforated tile. Measure the distance in feet around your foundation footing and that is the amount to buy, plus some additional feet for safety. (It's very inexpensive.) (NOTE: If you buy all your material from one source — either a building supply store or a materials yard — you can probably return all excess material for a full refund.)

You don't have to connect the drain tile. Lay the sections about an inch apart. When this is done, *carefully* fill in the bottom of the trench with gravel. Fill in about 6 inches to cover the top of the tile. Don't shovel the gravel down into the trench because you might break the waterproof seal that you have built along your foundation wall. In the event moisture does accumulate, it will now run into the tile which will act as a reservoir and allow the water to drain into the ground gradually.

The Last Step

There is one final step before you backfill, and that is to put up wallboard to protect your fragile, waterproofed wall. Wallboard usually comes in 4′ × 8′ or 4′ × 10′ sheets, although contractors also buy it in a 4′ × 20′ size. Building supply stores usually throw away the pieces with broken ends and frequently have a supply of damaged wallboard on hand. These are the pieces you can use and you might be able to get them free, or certainly at greatly reduced cost.

This is how to use the wallboard. Take your tape measure or a yardstick and measure from the top of the footing up to the point where you stopped tarring. (This will be the top of your backfill level.) Measure off that distance — let's say 5 feet — on a section of wallboard. Draw a pencil line and make your cut with an X-Acto knife. The wall-

board will break easily along the cut. Then lay that piece of wallboard against the tarred wall. It will probably stick there, and it doesn't have to be more secure than that because its only function is to act as a buffer to protect your foundation when you backfill. Cut as many pieces as you need, butting each sheet up against the next. Be careful not to put any holes in the foundation. If it doesn't stick, dab some tar spots on the back of the wallboard to provide adhesion.

It is best to backfill by hand, and you should take care not to shovel stones against your foundation. You obviously can't remove every stone, but you certainly don't want to throw in the big stones because if you break the water barrier, you're right back where you started before you got all that tar on your clothes. (This is a task where it pays to have friends. And the true friend is one who will not only shovel backfill but will also bring along his own shovel to do it.)

When all excavated sides of the foundation have been backfilled, you will have a lot of dirt left over, even after you pack down the backfilled area. That's because the dirt you removed was compacted and the backfill must be allowed to settle, which it will in a week or two. So don't move out your excess dirt. And don't use water to soak it down. You might also notice that some of the wallboard is sticking up above the backfill level. That can easily be removed with your X-Acto knife. The buried wallboard will disintegrate in time and the worst that could happen is that the lime could sweeten your soil.

SUMMARY

- Hire backhoe operator to dig trench around foundation. (Check out and mark lines and pipes leading from house.) Dig outer wall at an angle to prevent cave-in. Dig trench 2½ feet wide and 4 inches below top of foundation footing.
- Wire brush dirt from foundation wall.

- Fill cracks and leaky joints with mortar.
- Apply layer of mortar at angle between bottom of foundation wall and concrete footing.
- Apply foundation covering on wall.
- Put up fiberglass membrane on sticky tar surface of wall; overlap strips.
- Apply layer of tar on top of fiberglass mesh.

- Lay drainage tile at base of footing.
- Cover with gravel (carefully).
- Put up wallboards against waterproofed wall around entire foundation for protection against backfill.
- Backfill — by hand.

WATER PROBLEMS WITH A CONCRETE SLAB FLOOR

TOOLS & MATERIALS NEEDED

- ☐ Shovel
- ☐ Trowel
- ☐ Wire brush
- ☐ Mortar
- ☐ Foundation covering
- ☐ Old paintbrush (for tar)
- ☐ Concrete blocks
- ☐ Cord, stakes, hammer
- ☐ Wire mesh

Build a Flash Wall

Outside the snowbelt, many homes are built on concrete slabs. Homeowners usually plant flower gardens or shrubs against the sides of their homes and often, over a period of years, soil piles up over the sill. Moisture then causes the sill to deteriorate and the paint on the baseboard inside the house will often peel. The sill is a treated piece of 2″ × 4″ lumber which is bolted to the concrete foundation.

The soil should be at least six inches below the level of your first floor, and water should be able to drain away from the house. If the water *doesn't* drain properly, you can't correct it by changing the slope of the soil. But you *can* build a flash wall that will solve the problem — permanently.

First, remove the dirt from the slab at the exterior of your house; dig down about 16 inches below the top of the slab. Your trench should extend at least 12 inches out from the house to allow you room to

work. Shovel the dirt back from the trench so you don't have to kneel in it, but keep it handy for backfill. (NOTE: You shouldn't run into any pipes when digging at this depth, but be careful anyway.) After your trench is dug and the dirt along the exposed side of the slab is dry, clean it off with a stiff bristle or wire brush. Then dust off the slab with an old paintbrush or rag.

The next step is to apply a coat of foundation coating on the concrete or stucco foundation. You can buy foundation coating at your hardware store. It is usually sold in 5-gallon cans, and it's essentially tar in a can. You can apply it as is. Use a three-knot brush designed for this kind of job or a 4-inch or wider paintbrush — an old one — because you won't be able to paint with it again. Let the foundation coating set for a few hours and then give it a second coat.

Now lay a foundation of cement or concrete at the bottom of the trench; it should be about 4 to 6 inches deep and at least as wide. Keep it out about 2 inches from the wall. When it has set, build your first course of concrete blocks along this foundation.

Most concrete blocks measure 8″ or 6″ or 4″ × 8″ × 16″ and have two or three hollow cores. They're built to stack and should be laid with the cores running vertically. Before mortaring, place one block at each end of the foundation and drive a wood stake in the dirt at either end just in front of them. Then run a taut, sturdy mason's line between the two stakes, even with the tops of your blocks. This will give you the proper height so you can build a level wall. After you apply your mortar, each block should just fit level with your line. If a block is too high, tap it down; if it is too low, use

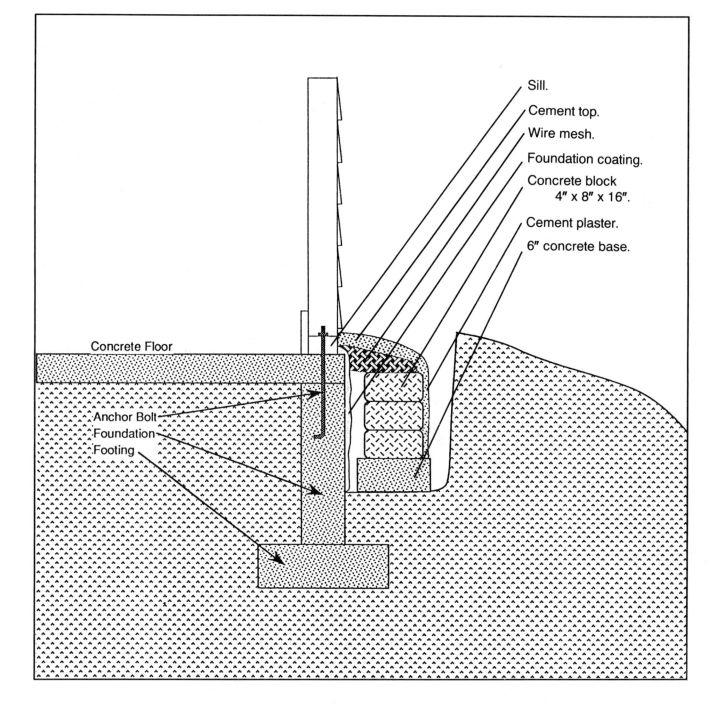

more mortar in your joint. To make doubly sure, use a level as you work.

Allow Dead Air

When you start your first course, don't lay your concrete blocks flush against the foundation slab. Keep your concrete block wall about 1½ inches out from the foundation. You do this to provide a dead air space which will help to kill any moisture seeping through your wall. After your first course has been laid, start the second row. You might even have to build three courses high because the tops of your blocks should be about 3 or 4 inches above the ground after you have backfilled. Incidentally, since most of the wall is underground, you can be as sloppy with your mortar as you like. When the wall has been completed, apply a coat of cement on the front (the outside) and let it set for a day.

The next step is to paint a layer of foundation coating (tar) over the newly cemented side of your wall to waterproof it. Then lay a strip of wire mesh between the top of your wall and the side of your house. The wire mesh comes in strips about 8 feet long and 4 inches wide and is bent into an "L". Plasterers use this type of wire mesh in the corners when they are plastering a room. You can buy it at a hardware or building supplies store.

Cut as much as you need and bend it to form a little roof over the dead air space. This is done to keep the cement from falling down into the air space between your wall and the slab when you cover it over with mortar. Slant your "roof" so that when rainwater comes down the exterior wall, it will run away from the house to the outside of your wall. Also make sure the wire mesh is completely cov-

ered over with mortar because it will rust if exposed. (Later, you can paint the exposed areas with the same color paint as the rest of your house to make it look neat.)

Allow a day or two for the mortar to harden, then backfill the dirt, and your water problems should be history.

Since you will be kneeling in the dirt for most of this job, it will be worth your while to invest in a pair of knee guards. Carpetlayers often wear them and most garden shops sell them as well. Or, since a lot of the kids now use them for skateboarding, maybe you can borrow a pair.

SUMMARY

- Remove dirt from slab; dig about 16 inches below the top of the slab. Trench should be about 12 inches out from the house. Keep dirt for backfill.
- Clean away dirt from stucco with wire brush and apply two coats of foundation coating (tar).
- Lay 6-inch foundation of concrete at the bottom of the trench.
- Build cinderblock wall on concrete foundation. Stay out 1½ inches from slab to provide dead air space.
- Cement side of wall and cover cement with foundation coating when dry.
- Cover top of dead air space with wire mesh and cover this with mortar and foundation covering.
- Backfill with original soil.

"I'VE GOT ROCKS IN MY HOUSE"

Restoring an old house is like raising kids: by the time you learn how, it's too late. And even though it is an experience you probably wouldn't care to repeat, it usually does turn out well. It also builds character and, if your marriage survives, it is surely one that no man can put asunder.

My partner Ed has spent a lifetime working with brick and stone. I got into it about eighteen years ago when we purchased an old rock house in Galena, Illinois. The following is an article I wrote for the *Chicago Tribune Magazine* back in 1972 when I was working in an advertising agency in Chicago. One word of explanation: The prices will seem incredibly modest compared with those in today's marketplace. You should also be reminded that this was also before Los Angeles real estate prices went through the roof. (I should know — my Encino home sold for a fraction of the $300,000-plus that it's worth today.)

There's also an update to the article. What began as an, "I don't know why the heck we bought it purchase," is now our home and was a part of the Galena Tour of Antique Homes two years ago, when 2600 people went through on a weekend.

About five years ago we decided to build a one-room addition on the east side of the rock house, to balance out the turn-of-the-century brick kitchen addition on the west side. The kitchen has a porch on the front; we reversed it on the addition by adding a screened-in porch in the back with a sliding glass door that opens up on the porch. We also added a flagstone patio behind the house. These relatively modest additions cost more than the initial price and restoration expense of the original house.

As a historical footnote, General Grant returned home to Galena after the Civil War but left soon after to become President. When the town was young, back in 1826, it was larger than Chicago and the site of the most important lead mines in the nation, as well as the biggest riverboat port north of St. Louis. It might still be forgotten if the Branniger Company hadn't bought a number of farms in a scenic valley and started selling lots and building second homes for city dwellers, in addition to building a lake and two championship golf courses.

When several million dollars was spent on Chicago television advertising the "life in the country" charms of The Galena Territory, just outside "historic Galena," the secret was out. And even though our major effort is tourism, Jo Daviess County still has the greatest number of dairy cows in Illinois. With a Galena population of 4,000, that's probably more cows than people . . . not counting tourists.

My Story

So here you are. Three hours out of Chicago. Driving along on your first trip to Galena. Navigator/wife in the bucket seat to the right, kids in the jumping seat aft, and a picnic lunch in the trunk. Suddenly: "There it is," screams your wife. "To the right. Just what we've been looking for."

You make a sudden stop. Not a panic stop but still a complete surprise to the driver of the tailgating milk truck who has been trying to gain momentum to climb the modest grade, around the blind curve of the narrow, shoulderless, blacktop road. Somehow he manages to pull past you and, in the same

The stairs looked so crazy we figured they had to be saved.

There were no antiques in the attic except maybe the blurry panes in the windows and the roof, which leaked.

The original walls were coated with a mixture of limestone and sand with cow hair for a binder. The previous owners did the removal, which had to be a tough job.

Like the real estate man said, "It had possibilities."

The exterior ground level in back was about 5 feet above the interior floor level, so the wall leaked. What looks like a second story privy was a kind of kitchenette.

Still lots of work to be done, but this is how it looks now.

moment, avoid another truck coming down the hill.

No thanks to you, everyone avoids getting crushed, but then, if you hadn't stopped you probably wouldn't have bought the house. What house? The old rock house on the hill to the right. The one your wife said . . . there it was. Just what you were looking for.

Well anyway, that's pretty much how it happened with us. We went up for the first time on Memorial Day and bought the house on the second trip, the Fourth of July. There's no significance to the days. It just happened that way four years ago.

When we first saw it, the house was vacant. Maybe abandoned is a better word. Certainly in obvious need of repairs. But, as the real estate people say, it had possibilities. The house was built in the side of a hill; constructed of native limestone dug from its own quarry. To the left was attached a small, one-room, brick kitchen, painted an off-lichen color. There was a separate, two-story garage to the left of the kitchen. Off to the right of the house was a big, wide, sloping lawn. And above the house, growing out of the steep limestone outcropping, was a beautiful old elm tree sheltering the entire scene. Hey, maybe this was what I was looking for after all.

Why did I want an old, broken down house 160 miles away from our apartment in Evanston? Well, we had just moved to the Chicago area from Los Angeles, in the San Fernando Valley, where we had our own house and lawn and pool and garden. All of which my wife took care of. I was deeply concerned that she wouldn't like our move to a Midwest apartment because she wouldn't have enough to do. A little house where she could putter around on weekends would be just the thing for her.

When I told her that I planned to buy the place, Kay was deeply concerned, too. She said simply, "You're insane."

Coming from California, where a "no-money-down" purchase of a new house is a way of life and where real estate agents earn a living by selling the same lot back and forth to each other, I felt like Reddy Fox in the henhouse. With all those depressed land values, I could smell a land boom about to burst. So I figured I'd buy the house like a used car. A few bucks down and a few more each month. I could always sell out at a fat profit when property started to zoom in the next few months.

What I didn't know was that Galena already had had its land boom. Back in 1828. That's when prospectors swarmed in to get the lead mines going some five years before Chicago was incorporated.

As it says in the excellent Federal Writers Project book, *Illinois* (917.73 in your library): "While other settlements were building log cabins, Galena was erecting the mansions of stone and brick which still mark a high level in America's architectural development. While settlers in other regions were concerned with the struggle for existence, Galena's citizens were building churches and schools, founding a library . . . and altogether living a life unmatched in the Middle Border."

But after a while the lead mines gave out, the Galena River silted up, and the railroads moved in. Since then, the years have worn well. Time has been kind. It ignored the town completely. Now, I was going to turn back the clock.

When we decided to buy the house, I had a property lawyer friend in Chicago call the real estate man in Galena to complete the deal. We had already agreed to a price of $5,000, with a cash down payment of $1,500 and the balance by contract purchase. I still don't know what happened. Maybe the real estate man didn't like lawyers, or maybe just my friend, but he called to say that the sale was off unless I dealt with him direct. Like any other sharp businessman, I said, "Why not?"

Next weekend we went to the home of one of the bank officers, and the real estate man explained the nature of the deal and the size of the loan. The banker asked, "What are you doing to do with the house?" I said, "Fix it." He said, "Are you working?" I said, "Yup." He said, "Okay. I'll send the papers out in the morning." Which he did: $3,500 at 6½ percent interest, payable at $50 per month over a five-year period, with the unpaid balance due on the last installment.

Except for the last few years, the house had been lived in continuously. The most recent owners were a couple of guys who, for a.short while, ran an antique store in town. They had planned to restore the place but abandoned the project when they found what it would cost. They especially wanted to install a fireplace but realized that it would destroy the interior look as well as the exterior lines of the house. So they left town.

The first time we took a close look at what we had taken on, Kay started to cry. It seemed possible that we had purchased total disaster.

The previous owners had stripped most of the house down to the bare rock walls. It was a necessary preliminary, but the result was not lovely to look upon. In the kitchen (which had been added to the basic building later) they had pried and peeled off plaster from the back wall, revealing the original brick. The front and side walls looked as if our boys had beaten on the plaster with every kind of hand tool known to demolition science. The interior walls in most older houses were made of sand and lime mixed with water and cow or horse hair for a binder. But this stuff seemed a lot tougher than that. The floor was pretty well rotted. As we found out later, it had been laid on the top of a limestone shelf footing.

From the kitchen, moving right, we went through a doorway 20 inches deep — the thickness of the exterior walls — and entered the living room. It was the only room downstairs. Once there had been two, but our fireplace boys had removed the dividing wall. We intended to leave it that way.

Right now, the windows wouldn't open, the back wall was wet, the ceiling sagged, and the pine floor bulged. The stairs were steep and narrow but charming in a funky kind of way. You took the first step facing the back wall, then the next couple of steps wheeled you right 90 degrees to the second floor.

There were two bedrooms. The walls of the west room were stripped down to the old-fashioned wood-lath supports. In the floor was a square hole, which had once housed a register, to let the heat rise from below. The plaster in the other room was still intact, but the sagging hardboard ceiling was a foot lower.

In the ceiling of the west room was a trapdoor, the entrance to the attic. Kay said: "Let's get a ladder and you can hand down the four-poster beds and other goodies that are probably stored there. I don't want to go up — I thought I heard a bat."

I took a look. There was easy standing room at the highest point. The roof sloped sharply toward the eaves. At the east end were two small windows; at the west, a brick chimney. But no goodies. I could see a couple of broken chairs, some junk clothes, and assorted debris. The most noticeable thing was bat dung. The fumes burned my eyes. What seemed like a million bats screamed, "Get out." So I did.

Back in the city, we began to think about what we had. Or, more accurately, what we didn't have.

First, we didn't have water. We did have a cistern. It was a nice one, about 20 or 30 feet deep, round, brick lined, and toped with a broken pump.

They tell me the fire department used to come around a couple times a year to fill the cistern with fresh water. This was pumped into buckets and used for cooking, clothes washing, and bathing. People nearby us still live this way. Some houses have a downspout that takes rain water from the roof into the cistern. I don't know how this stuff mixes with booze, but I hear it's great for washing your hair. We haven't tried it yet. We never got the pump fixed, and last year someone stole it.

Next, we didn't have heat. The bigger houses in Galena, particularly those influenced by Federal, New Orleans, or Greek Revival design, had fireplaces but often as much for show as for warmth. Once Ben Franklin invented his stove, nobody wanted a fireplace (except our predecessors). So we inherited a big, square coal and wood-burning stove in the living room. It was left there because nobody could lift it. The junk man wanted $20 to haul it away.

Next, our electrical wiring had been done by Mickey Mouse. Even so, there was a TV outlet, and the local television repair shop owner said he'd sell me a set any time and "all's I have to do is plug it in."

Needless to say, we didn't have a john. An outhouse, yes. It was demurely screened from the road by a clump of lilac bushes. A two-seater. But the door wouldn't close.

The cellar was a bigger mess than the attic. Apparently it had been used originally as the kitchen and was about two-thirds the size of the living room directly above. The cellar walls had the same native limestone construction as the exterior walls. We entered through a trapdoor in the front porch floor, went down a flight of old wooden steps and through a thick, solid plank, tomahawkproof door. In recent years the room had been used to store home-canned preserves. Now the shelves had been torn from the walls and the floor was covered inches deep with broken Mason jars. I've seen tidier disaster areas.

We made periodic trips to Galena the first year, wondering where to start, or indeed if we should start at all. Amazingly, no one had any really helpful advice. Everyone who had restored an old house felt that the only procedure to follow was the one he had used, but of course each circumstance was different. There was a pattern, though. Some-

how each had contrived to fix up one room to sleep in and then had taken on the rest of the house. It made sense, but not for use. For one thing, our roof leaked. There were also those bats. We couldn't keep them out because there were too many holes.

A kind of process of elimination and a reluctant resort to common sense set up our restoration schedule. It had to be top down and outside in. More simply, we weatherproofed the house.

It was now one year later. We had found an architect to help us before we started. His family lived in town, but he worked in Chicago and returned weekends. Unfortunately, he was in the process of changing jobs and couldn't design our complete plans, but we were able to consult with him on each step.

Step one was a new roof over the top of the existing roof, which turned out to be 1-inch planking after the shingles were removed. Over this we put 1-inch exterior plywood and new shingles.

If there was a local contractor who could handle all the various phases of building or reconstruction, I couldn't find him. Consequently, I followed the procedure used by most out-of-towners in restoring their Galena homes. Each job has to be negotiated separately with a plumber, carpenter, or whoever. He will estimate the job and, if given a go-ahead, complete the work to his personal satisfaction and bill you. The owner is usually on the premises when the job is in progress so that he can supervise the workmanship. However, I had to issue instructions via the long-distance telephone and the U.S. mail. Naturally, all work was unsupervised.

About this time I invented a little game which I call construction-trade roulette. You take a fully loaded industrial stapler, hold it to your forehead, and pull the trigger. Any staple, of course, will hurt beyond belief. But it's a game of chance because every sixth staple is painted red.

To be truthful, almost everything worked out surprisingly well. Along with a new roof we put up white painted aluminum gutters, downspouts, and concrete splash pads; cost $1,327.67. We also put in new six-light windows downstairs; cost $333.56. They looked the same, except the new ones could open. The upstairs windows still retained many of the original panes with the blurry glass, and I thought it might be a nice thing to save them.

If the roof didn't leak anymore, the back wall in the living room did. Water seeped through because the earth level outside was about 5 feet higher than the floor level inside. Once there had been a walkway behind the house, but through the years rubble and runoff from the limestone shelves above packed in solid against the wall.

It would have been fairly easy to dig out the fill and restore the walkway, but I felt it would be better to make enough room for a patio. Unfortunately, the limestone shelf extended farther out than we had thought. I got the space I wanted by blasting. The biggest blast came when I got the bill — $850. But it looks good.

Now that the back wall didn't leak any more and spring was upon us, we made an honest effort to repair the upstairs windows. I had a fellow try to replace the broken glass with some new old glass from the downstairs windows. No way. Not without breaking the window frames, too. So we replaced all the upstairs windows. Cost — $250.73.

Next we contracted with a stonemason to sandblast the exterior of the house, including the brick kitchen. Later, he tuckpointed the entire house. He did a beautiful job, finished on time, and for the estimated amount. We also had him sandblast the interior brick wall at the back of the kitchen and one interior side rock wall in the living room, both of which we planned to leave exposed. Then we fixed the chimneys and put stovepipe plugs where the openings had been. The cost for all this was $1,817.72.

Now the entire house was absolutely weatherproof. But not batproof. Maybe the bats liked it where they were or maybe they couldn't get out, but I vividly remember watching a wave of the squeaking creatures climb up behind the exposed laths in the bedroom toward the attic. And suddenly that was the last of them. We haven't seen or heard one since. Sorry, Dracula.

I learned that nothing happens immediately, or even soon, in the construction business. For me it was always the "busy season." For instance, I put in my request for a well in January and it was finally dug in the last week of August. But I'm sure not complaining, because we struck water at about 40 feet and went down an additional 40 feet to assure a good, steady flow. The entire job cost much less ($387) than I had figured, and the water is great.

But I found that after you've drilled a well, you're still a long way from a cold drink of water. First we had to install a submersible pump, run a copper pipe underground from the well through the wall of the cellar to an 80 gallon pressure tank, and finally to wire the entire system electrically so that it works automatically. All at a cost of $575. And still not a drop to drink. No electricity, that's why.

Wiring the house became the next project. We were lucky to find a local electrician who told me he could work only part time, between other commitments and on weekends. It took almost half a year, but here we were in no hurry because so many other things had to be done. He wouldn't accept a cent until the entire job was completed. The bill was $562; once again, good news.

While our electrician was working part time, we had a plumbing contractor working full time. At least I had this pipe dream that it would turn out that way. Unfortunately, he soon became bogged down. He started asking silly questions like approximately where did we want to install the bathroom.

Our first thought had been to build a new room upstairs, outside the original house. The exorbitant cost quickly killed that idea. Finally we thought small and came up with a plan to build a little hall to the right at the top of the stairs. A door to the left and one to the right would open into adjoining bedrooms. We then stole 5 feet from the east bedroom and put up a new wall, giving us a 5′ × 9′ bathroom; just big enough for a 5′ × 5′ square bathtub.

Our plumber was able to get started now. And that's as far as he got. In a stone house everything is exposed. There is nowhere to hide things like wires and pipes. Since we had no closets and no room to install any, we had decided to build a storage area against the back wall in the living room and to panel this space with 2-foot wide pine floorboard from the attic. The exposed pipes from the future bathroom directly overhead could be neatly hidden behind this wall. Vertically, then, no problem. Horizontally, something else again. These pipes had to run the length of the house, buried under the floor. Starting at the spot where we planned to put a kitchen sink, the pipe had to run through the living room, dipping deeper on a slant as it went, to provide a gravity flow. In most houses this is not a problem because it runs through the basement or sometimes the crawl space. Unfortunately, the rear third of the original house and the entire kitchen were perched on that damn limestone ledge.

So we tore up the kitchen floor and discarded the rotten floorboards. The pine boards in the living room were usable. Next we had a trench dug. Every inch of the way with a jackhammer. Incidentally, the only things of value found beneath the kitchen floor were a Civil War vintage marble and a Wm. Rogers Bros. nickel silver teaspoon that someone had used to stir paint.

The city sewer doesn't run as far as our house. And now that we had that neat pipe lying there, we figured that we'd better lead it somewhere. Like to a septic tank. No big deal at most places. A huge, preformed concrete box is dropped into a hole dug in the ground. Your pipe runs underground from the house into the tank, and a drain field is constructed on the outlet side. But you don't do it easily when you're working on top of a stone quarry. It cost $750 to do it the hard way.

And so we were ready to get at the bathroom. I went into a showroom on Michigan Avenue and ordered bathroom fixtures like a kid buying penny candy; one of these, one of those, and two of them. My plumber couldn't install anything until the walls were up, but that didn't matter because delivery was held up for a couple of months. The truck strike was on. (Final price when completed, including plumbing and bathroom — $1,231.03.)

At this point the kitchen floor was exposed dirt. An open trench ran across the back third of the living room. Floorboards and tools were everywhere else, and complete despair and misery were upon us. We felt lower than the bottom of our septic tank. We were about halfway finished, and completion seemed far beyond the horizon. We had invested a fair amount financially and emotionally, and all we had to show for it was bare walls, dirt floors, exposed pipes and wires, and a couple of holes in the ground. No one in his right mind would have given us 3 cents for the entire mess, and I doubt if the bank would have taken it back as a gift. Then things got worse.

Since there was no turning back, we had nowhere else to go but forward. While the floors were torn up, we made arrangements to put in heat. We checked out an electrical system which would have been easy to install but costly to maintain. The most practical method for us seemed to be a gas furnace with forced air. In a word, this means ducts. The furnace was placed in the cellar, and most of the ducts ran under the floor or behind the storage wall. The kitchen duct was laid in sand and waterproofed on the limestone shelf, then later buried in the concrete slab. The cost — $1,230.

It was about then that everything started falling apart. Heating, plumbing, and electrical work was halted until we could put up walls. We found a carpenter/contractor and made arrangements to rebuild the interior of the house, then told each man to synchronize his actions with the other. Now, with everything set on "Go," the elm tree died and I lost my job.

I was in deep, of course, but I reasoned that at the rate my team was going, they'd never finish anyway. The electric people had informed me that they wouldn't allow their system to be installed unless the house was properly insulated. When we decided to go with gas, we were indoctrinated on the need to "seal out the cold." After the basic firring out was completed, rock wool insulation was put in. Then we had drywall ceilings and walls installed. I had wanted to go with plaster but was talked out of it.

Then suddenly the heating man finished, the electrician finished, the bathroom was completed, and all the walls were put up and the floors down. Fortunately, by now, I had another job and was only financially ruined when I paid the bills: construction, $2,732.50; materials $1,359.61. And finally we added a water heater, $124.03 installed.

At this point all of the basic work is done. We still have to finish the floors and woodwork, fix the stairs, paper the bedroom walls, put in the back living room wall, paint the remaining walls, install the kitchen sink, and miscellaneous other things. Like buying antique pine furniture for the entire place. So far, the total cost breaks down like this:

Rock House Cost

Cost of house (not including 6½ percent interest on $3,500 for four years)	$5,000.00
Roof and downspouts	1,327.67
Windows, upstairs and downstairs	584.26
Excavation	850.00
Tuckpointing and sandblasting	1,817.72
Well	387.00
Pump and pressure tank	575.00
Electricity	562.00
Plumbing including bathroom	1,231.03
Septic tank	750.00
Heat	1,230.00
Carpentry	2,732.61
Materials for carpentry work	1,359.61
New footing for kitchen, closing in bathroom doorway; materials	177.97
Water heater	124.03
Total to date	$18,708.82

Allowing approximately $6,500 for completing the interior, fixing the porch, making a one-story structure of the garage, and tying in the roof with the house and basic landscaping, the overall cost will run about $25,000.

Is it worth the effort? Well, I've learned a few things about that. Restoring an old house is an emotional endeavor with deep psychological roots. With some people apparently it fulfills a need to tie in with the historical past, a turning back of the clock, if you will. Other people perhaps feel that they have made a down payment on immortality. I suppose, at one time or another, there is always the thought that, "Now the Joneses will have to keep up with me." But that's short-lived. The Joneses pity you, your fellow participants in the cult sympathize with you, and the natives forever suspect you. They really wonder, "Why?" A future retirement house is an easy cop-out explanation. It wouldn't be true for us. I have a simple geographic retirement philosophy: sunshine beats snowballs.

Actually, it's a pretty lousy investment although it can act as an enforced savings plan. If you're lucky, you get most of your money back. In my own case, it was probably a need to put down roots; to belong. Maybe also because I grew up in a small, forgotten town. But then as a kid, my sole ambition in life was to get away. My wife has neatly solved the entire complex equation. She says, "You're nuts."

Probably so.

I have been looking at another place up the street. It's even more dilapidated than our house ever was. But with what I know now, I can probably do it in half the time and at half the cost.

Section III
Appendix

Glossary
Resources

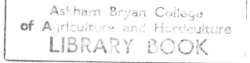

GLOSSARY

ANCHOR BOLT — L-shaped metal bolt embedded in foundation to anchor sill of house to foundation.

BED JOINT — Horizontal layer of mortar at the bottom of a brick or block.

BOND — Mortar bond: the adhesion between brick and mortar. Pattern bond: the arrangement of bricks used in a wall, walk, or other surface.

BRICK — A building block, of oblong shape, made of clay fired in a kiln. Standard size is 8″ × 2¼″ × 3¾″.

BRICK SET — Wide chisel for cutting bricks.

CEMENT — A powdered substance made of burned lime and clay, mixed with sand and water to make mortar.

COLD CHISEL — Used for cutting brick, block, or stone. Made with special steel to withstand metal-on-metal blows without splintering.

CONCRETE — A mixture of cement, sand, and gravel to which water has been added.

CONCRETE BLOCK — Used in construction of foundations and walls. Usually hollow, with two or three cells, made of concrete and fine cinders. (Also called cinderblock.)

CONCRETE GLUE — Used to increase the bond between bricks and mortar.

DRAIN TILE — Plastic pipe or flexible tubing used to carry off water. Can be perforated or watertight.

FINISH FLOAT — A board with a handle for smoothing off concrete after it has been poured.

FOUNDATION COATING — A tar-like substance used for waterproofing masonry.

GROUT — A mortar, generally mixed so it pours or flows easily, used for concrete, brick, and tile work in addition to crack repairs.

HAWK — A flat square piece of metal or wood, with a carrying handle on one side, used for holding mortar.

HEAD JOINT — The vertical layer of mortar at the sides of a brick or block.

HOD — A wood or metal trough with a long carrying handle, used for carrying mortar or bricks.

HUNT'S PROCESS — A liquid wax sprayed on newly poured concrete to seal in the moisture. This slows down the drying process and eliminates the need to spray water to prevent cracking. The wax is tinted to show which areas have been covered. Tint can be washed off after concrete is dry.

JOINT — The layer of mortar between bricks, blocks, or stone.

JOINTER — A long metal tool used in making mortar joints. There are various types, such as rat-tail jointer.

JOINT RAKER — A "scorpion," which is essentially a piece of wood with a nail that is used to rake out mortar joints to expose the full block or brick, rather than tooling the joint with a rat-tail jointer.

KUMALONG — A rake-like tool for smoothing a large expanse of cement, as with walks, floors, or pavements.

LINE BLOCK — Device that hooks on the end of a brick to hold mason's line. Use one at each end brick as the course is being laid.

LINE STRETCHER — Metal device for hooking onto the side of a concrete block to hold mason's line. Use one at each end block as the course is being laid.

MASON'S CHISEL — Designed for cutting brick, cinderblock, and stone.

MASON'S HAMMER — Designed with flat surface on one end, tapered on the other, for chipping.

MASON'S LEVEL — Similar to carpenter's level, with bubbles for determining true levels for brick or block, horizontally and vertically. Comes in several sizes. Small version called "torpedo."

MASON'S LINE — A horizontal line, used to keep courses of bricks level. A sturdy cord between two pins or stakes.

MASONRY MIX — A cement which includes lime, formulated for making mortar to be used for laying bricks.

MASONRY NAIL — A very strong nail, designed to penetrate masonry without bending.

MASTIC — A paste-like substance used for sticking thin brick facing and tiles. It comes premixed in gallon cans and is usually applied with a notched trowel. Available in building and tile supply stores.

MORTAR — A mixture of sand, cement, and water used to bond brick, block, or stone.

PAVER — A type of brick, generally used for walks or driveways.

PLUMB LINE — A vertical line.

PORTLAND CEMENT — A dry powder mixed with sand and water to make mortar, and with the addition of gravel to make concrete. Usually sold in 97-pound (1 cubic foot) paper sacks.

READY MIX — Concrete, ready for pouring, delivered by special truck. Also called transit mix.

REBAR — (Reinforcing bar) Steel for reinforcing block walls and concrete footings.

SCAFFOLD — Sturdy (usually 2-inch) wood planking, supported by steel pipe framework which can be disassembled for transporting. Used by bricklayers for working above 5-foot heights.

SCORPION — See JOINT RAKER.

SCREED — A solid wood or metal tool for smoothing sand prior to laying a brick walk or pathway. It has a notched end on either side to fit over forms.

SPACER — Device used to keep uniform spaces between bricks or tile.

STUCCO — A fine or coarse plaster or cement used for plastering interior or exterior walls.

TORPEDO — See MASON'S LEVEL.

TROWEL — A flat metal tool, usually triangular in shape, used for applying mortar to bricks or blocks.

TUCKPOINTER — Specialized tool used in tuckpointing work.

TUCKPOINTING — To clean out the old mortar in joints between brick or stone and replace with new mortar.

TUCKPOINTING CHISEL — Narrow chisel used for cutting away soft or deteriorated bricks prior to repair.

WIRE BRUSH — A brush with wire bristles, used for brushing bricks or stonework.

WOLMANIZE — Process used to pressure-treat lumber to reduce deterioration due to weather or embedding in soil. Wolmanized lumber is used for 2″ × 4″ forms left in soil.

RESOURCES

Books

Advanced Masonry. Alexandria, VA: Time-Life Books, Inc., 1982.

How to Build Walks, Walls, Patio Floors. 2nd ed. Menlo Park, CA: Lane Book Co., 1963.

Masonry. New York: Time, Inc., 1976.

Brimer, John Burton. *Homeowner's Complete Outdoor Building Book: Wood and Masonry Construction.* New York: Popular Science Books, 1985.

Dalzell, Ralph J. and Gilbert Townsend. *Masonry Simplified.* 3rd ed. Chicago: American Technical Society, 1973.

Day, Richard. *The Practical Handbook of Concrete and Masonry.* New York: Arco Publishing Co., 1969.

Huff, Darrell. *How to Work with Concrete and Masonry.* New York: Popular Science Publishing Co., 1968.

Kreh, Richard T., Sr. *Masonry Skills.* New York: Van Nostrand Reinhold Company, Inc., 1976.

— *Mastering Advanced Masonry Skills.* 2nd ed. New York: Van Nostrand Reinhold Company, Inc., 1983.

Russell, James E. *Walks, Walls and Fences.* Passaic, NJ: Creative Homeowner Press, 1981.

Articles

Fossel, P. J. "Design and Lay a Flagstone Walk." *Americana,* May-June 1987, pp. 63-5.

Gould, A. R. "Pave the Way." *Workbench,* July/August 1988, pp. 34-6.

"Three Walks that Work." *Southern Living,* November 1988, p. 76.

Government Publications

The following publications may be available in your library or through the U.S. Government Printing Office, Superintendent of Documents, Washington, DC 20402.

Grimmer, Anne E., compiler. *A Glossary of Historic Masonry Deterioration Problems and Preservation Treatments.* U.S. Government Printing Office, 1984.

Mack, Robert C., *Repointing Mortar Joints in Historic Brick Buildings.* U.S. Government Printing Office, 1977.

INDEX